Praise for

The Art of Slicing Work

"Anton's book is beautifully written with real-world examples that will inspire you to think differently about the possible ways you can change the structure of your work and deliver value more quickly."

—HOWARD SUBLETT, former CEO of Scrum Alliance Inc.

"I was responsible for cofounding a new countrywide government institution in an environment of high volatility. Anton's knowledge helped me to set up more flexible and adaptable structures. I am glad to see it condensed into a book."

—KATARINA PERANIĆ, Director of the German Foundation for Commitment and Volunteering

"Anton is a continuous source of inspiration and knowledge on organizing our work. Through his principles, we have learned to organize ourselves as an organization in such a way that we can much better and more quickly advocate for climate policies that assure a safer and more livable future."

—ROSA BRANDT, Cofounder of Future Matters

"Anton is on a mission to bring new ways of working, and effective ways of organizing and leading, to new contexts. We've known each other for years, training leaders together, who mostly come from an IT background. The key to making 'agile' work is thinking differently about the work so that we can break it up into different pieces—into different kinds of pieces. If we do this right, it enables us to change the way we work together. Anton has framed the approach to breaking up work into the 'right' kind of pieces in a way that works outside of software and can be understood by people outside of IT.

With this book, Anton is taking the essential piece of what we've been doing in software in the last twenty years, stripping it of all buzzwords, and explaining it in clear language that everyone can understand."

—OLAF LEWITZ, Trust Artist and Certified Enterprise Coach

The Art of Slicing Work

The Art of Slicing Work

How To Navigate Unpredictable Projects

Anton Skornyakov

This is a work of creative nonfiction. Some parts have been fictionalized in varying degrees, for various purposes.

First Edition

Internal illustrations by Virpi Oinonen
Cover art by Liz Driesbach
Graphic from Paket/Shutterstock.com
Internal design by Jillian Rahn
Author photograph by Izzy Dempsey

ISBN 978-3-9826092-0-1 (ebook)
ISBN 978-3-9826092-1-8 (paperback)
ISBN 978-3-9826092-2-5 (hardcover)

Published by Agile.Coach GmbH & Co. KG
https://agile.coach/

Contents

Introduction

Alan works for a prominent health food manufacturer. He enjoys his work, and he loves his company's mission: to create tasty, cost-effective, and above all, *healthy* alternatives to common snack foods.

From time to time, new government regulations are set, and it's Alan's job to ensure that his company complies with them. He welcomes any opportunity to improve—he just wishes that he and his team were a little better at executing these projects.

To put it mildly, none of Alan's previous attempts to adapt his company to new regulations has felt particularly straightforward or productive. His team typically spends months on preparations only for unpredictable setbacks to occur during implementation. No matter how much time his team invests in planning, small and unintended consequences arise and compound over time. At the same time, because the company invests so much in preparation, they are reluctant to adapt their plans when issues inevitably arise. Eventually, they have to stretch the rules and put in incredibly long hours just to meet the implementation deadline. This stressful phase occurs so regularly at the end of a project that it's become known company-wide as "crunch time."

During crunch time, Alan and the rest of his team have to improvise in order to get their intended results. Often, this approach works, but the outcome is far from guaranteed. Moreover, working under such uncertainty is both exhausting and emotionally taxing. Even if the team delivers the project on time, it is hard to shake the feeling that they missed something or that they could have performed better. After all, it's hard to celebrate victories when it's unclear whether you've truly won.

Alan knows that he and his team have been following a broken process. Unfortunately, neither he nor anyone else at the company knows what else to do.

This is the dilemma leaders like Alan face every day. They see firsthand how traditional, outdated approaches to unpredictable projects waste time and resources, de-motivate team members, and ultimately lead to either delays or outright failure—yet they continue to practice them, hoping for better results. Then, when projects fail, they respond by trying to prepare even more thoroughly next time.

That approach doesn't make any sense when trying to manage an unpredictable project. If you find yourself in a hole, the solution isn't to keep digging. And yet, in my experience, that's exactly what many companies do.

Fortunately, there is a solution: change your relationship to unpredictability. Instead of trying to avoid surprises, structure your work so you can learn from and adapt your plans in response to them.

In this book, you will learn to do exactly that through a practice called *slicing work*.

What Is Slicing Work?

Slicing is the ability to break down your project into very small parts, or milestones, that you can deliver within a few weeks. These milestones aren't arbitrary. Each is focused on creating a result that can be tested in the real world, allowing you to provide your team members with meaningful feedback. The team is then able to deliver valuable parts of the project over time, which reduces risk.

In order to restructure—or slice—your work, you need to ask three fundamental questions:

1. What are the highest-risk aspects of this project?
2. What are the first results that could de-risk each of these aspects?
3. How can your team deliver these results as lightweight and fast as possible so that the company learns and the project moves forward?

Slicing changes all aspects of a project, from delegation to ownership to collaboration. It changes how we ensure quality and measure progress, resulting in a much more modern leadership style.

While most experts writing on unpredictability focus on changing culture or rethinking leadership, I've found that concrete and lasting change begins with slicing projects so that people pay attention to what matters most at any given time. As you will see in the following chapters, this shift in focus in turn drives a shift in leadership and culture. After all, a change in culture won't stick for long if no one sees real results.

That said, slicing is neither a silver bullet nor a

shortcut. Teams practicing this methodology still encounter difficulties and setbacks.

You can't plan your way out of unpredictability. Surprises *will* come up. However, when you expect that unpredictable events will happen, you no longer have to waste time with detailed planning. Instead, you're able to use these moments of unpredictability to learn and adapt. Such an approach not only increases your team's chances of success, but it also creates a more productive—and enjoyable—place to work.

A Methodology Built on Experience

I've always been passionate about how human systems are designed and what helps them thrive. Both my master's degree in mathematics and my diploma in physics focused on random—you could say unpredictable—processes. After realizing these fields were too theoretical for my taste, however, I decided to pursue business, earning my MBA and becoming a successful entrepreneur.

Talk about unpredictability. Every day, managing a startup is like walking into a building and fighting a large fire. But while the early years were challenging, I eventually found ways to better organize my teams so we could ride the storm of unpredictability with less stress and more success. Today, as a Certified Scrum Trainer and coach, I work with nonprofits and government organizations on slicing work so that they can improve their impact as well.

While the concept of slicing is rooted in Scrum (anyone who practices Scrum skillfully also practices slicing, whether they realize it or not), we will not be using that particular jargon in this book. Similarly, while Scrum is typically associated with the tech world, you will not find any stories or examples from software companies in this book. I wrote this book for everyday managers across *all* industries.

As you'll see in the stories and examples that follow, the principles of slicing apply whether you're organizing a private dinner party or structuring a multiyear project in a large corporation. These are fictional stories, but they are all drawn from my real-world experience coaching organizations. My hope is that you'll see yourself in some of them and that, in doing so, you'll begin to shift your own thinking.

Will the methodology described in this book challenge your understanding of how to structure and perform your work? Yes—that is my intent. But take heart: of the thousands of managers I've trained in the art of slicing, all were happy to take on this new challenge. As they and many others like them have discovered, the ability to act with competence and confidence in the face of unpredictability is an essential leadership trait not only now, but also will be in the decades to come.

This ability won't come overnight though. Slicing work is an art, and while this book will teach you the craft, you will only become an artist through practice.

In the chapters that follow, I will explain all the concepts you need to know to understand the principles of slicing work. Then, in the final chapter, I will give you the essential tools you need to begin executing. The more you practice and develop your ability, the easier slicing will become—and once you see the difference in your everyday work, you'll never want to stop.

Of course, as you work through the following chapters, I'll be there to support you. So if you're ready to master a new way of working, let's get started.

1

What It Means to Slice Work

It's the end of summer, and you want to throw a backyard dinner party for some of your friends and neighbors. You want to make sure everyone's comfortable and feels at home, so the first thing you do is come up with a menu, one that suits the carnivores and the vegetarians and even the gluten-free guests.

You've already shopped, so that part's done. But with just one day to do all of the prep and cooking—it's a typical Saturday, and your two kids are coming and going from soccer practices and playdates with friends—you wonder how you can best divide the tasks in order to have everything ready by the time your guests arrive.

There are two different lists you could make to organize the work that you've got to do. The first would simply itemize the individual dishes or components of a dish that *can be tasted*.

MENU

Appetizers

Guacamole	Hummus
Fresh tomato salsa	

Dinner

Burgers (beef and veggie)	Oven-roasted potatoes
	Greek salad

Dessert

Tiramisu

The other would include *everything you need to do* to make the items on your menu.

❏ Slice avocados	❏ Peel potatoes
❏ Halve limes	❏ Slice potatoes
❏ Chop cilantro	❏ Slice tomatoes
❏ Mince garlic	❏ Tear lettuce
❏ Dice onion	❏ Make burger patties

In other words, the first list, which shows you at a glance everything that you're planning to serve, is the macro view of the dinner party. The second one is a micro view of the party, showing the *actual steps* you need to take to prepare the dinner.

So far, this may look like a process you already know how to execute. After all, the prep work for a dinner party is relatively straightforward. However, we can organize increasingly complex and sophisticated work in much the same way—it's just a matter of learning how to slice it.

Horizontal and Vertical Slices of Work

In the dinner party example, you can easily see the difference between the first and the second list. "Guacamole" isn't the same as "Slice avocados," but they're related. You need to first do the *action* of slicing avocados to get to the *result* of guacamole.

Slicing avocados is a *step* or a *horizontal slice* of the work. Guacamole is the *finished product* or *vertical slice* of the work.

So slicing your dinner preparation vertically means breaking it up into individual dishes that can be tasted by your guests. Slicing it horizontally means breaking it down into different cooking activities.

A vertical slice is a result. When you have a vertical slice, you can receive feedback from people who don't know anything about its creation.

A horizontal slice is a necessary step. Any action you take is a horizontal slice of the work.

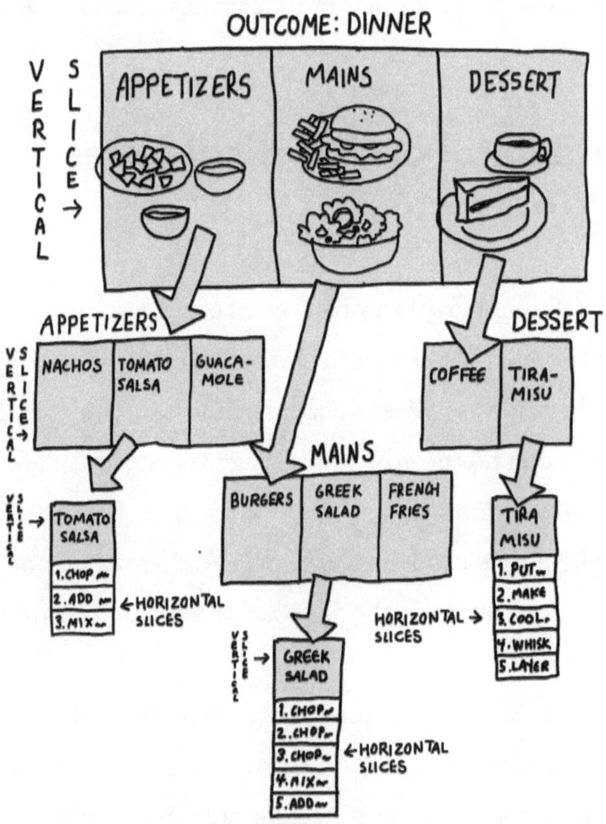

Fig. 1: Vertical and horizontal slicing in action.

Use One List to Change Scope

Which of the two lists helps you most when you want an overview of what's *going to be on the table* for your dinner party: the list outlining the entire menu or the one specifying individual tasks?

As we've discussed, the list with the menu represents the *finished product*—in this case, several different dishes—rather than the steps needed to create it. The list of individual steps doesn't help you quickly see what will be on the table, but the menu does. The menu represents the whole dinner preparation, sliced vertically.

In businesses, large projects often have only an extensive list of things that need to be done, such as things to analyze, research, or assemble—much like the horizontal list above. These lists show all of the tasks so they can be assigned to individuals or teams, but they don't give an overview. At the same time, the vertical lists of such projects are typically very coarse grained. They consist of only a few large milestones that can be tried out by customers.

Only the vertically sliced list gives you an overview of expected results, and only this list is helpful when you need to suddenly *change scope*.

Let's say you need to reduce your workload in order to

serve dinner at the planned hour. If you delete horizontal steps, you might save some prep time, but you'll negatively impact your result. For instance, not washing your knife after cutting meat is unsanitary, and cutting an ingredient or two from a particular dish will leave you with something no one wants to eat.

Fig. 2: Go ahead—try to change the scope of your dinner with a chaotic overview like this.

Luckily, there's a more straightforward way. That same vertical list that just showed you what will be on the table, the menu, is what you trim to *reduce scope*. You might make guacamole for the appetizer, ditch the hummus to save time, or make just one salad instead of two. Similarly, if five extra people show up, you can review the menu and adjust your choice of dishes to accommodate them.

We're talking about a dinner party, but the challenge of suddenly needing to change a project's scope happens all the time within organizations. Budgets shrink. Deadlines get moved. So learn to pivot by adjusting vertical slices.

Use the Other List to Assign Work

By now, it's early afternoon. Despite your now smaller-in-scope menu, you realize that you can't get all of these things cooked on your own, and you need to enlist some help. Your kids, eight and ten, are old enough to do simple things in the kitchen, but they still need guidance.

Which list do you pull from? Do you simply say, "Hey, you two, go make the guacamole" off the vertical list, or do you say, "Could you please peel the potatoes" from the horizontal one?

Fig. 3: Changing your scope is much easier with an overview like this.

Unless your kids just appeared on *Top Chef Jr.*, you'll probably hand them the potato peelers and ask them to stand over the sink so they don't make a big mess. Even then, you'll probably need to oversee the project: check their potato-peeling progress and give them feedback along the way.

On the other hand, your neighbor, who happens to be a professional chef, stops by to pick up her children and volunteers to pitch in. Do you give her a task from the vertical list or the horizontal one, like you did with your children? Of course, you'll give her a vertical slice, a complete item like guacamole or salsa, to make in its entirety because you know that she already has the skill set and the experience to accomplish that task without oversight.

What does all of this mean? While work can always be sliced vertically *and* horizontally, whom you delegate the work to will determine which slice you give them, and it will affect how you ensure quality.

The more skilled a person is, the more likely you'll assign them a vertical slice because you have a higher level of trust in them. Instead of constantly micromanaging their cooking, you check the quality of their work when the whole dish is done by tasting it, like a dinner guest.

On the other hand, less-experienced individuals should be assigned horizontal slices, which are closely monitored by others. It's important to note that those responsible for monitoring must be experts in the assigned tasks themselves, so they can effectively guide and course-correct the individuals they oversee along the way.

But Who Owns the Tomatoes?

Whether you slice work horizontally or vertically has an impact on the relationship between the person you've assigned the work to and the work itself. The single-minded tasks of horizontal slicing, like "slice tomatoes for the burgers," allow for ownership of the tomato slices, not the complete dish.

When my partner asks me to slice tomatoes, I usually ask her *how thin* she wants them sliced. By abdicating responsibility for the tomato slices, I'm shifting ownership back to her. But sometimes she'll say, "Think about it. You've eaten this dish ten times. You know how thin the tomatoes are usually sliced," which gives the ownership right back to me. The point is, when you give people small tasks, you're automatically *not* inviting them to own the whole thing, to think for themselves.

On the other hand, when I'm simply asked to make burgers, all the components become my responsibility. I own every piece of the process in this vertically sliced piece of work. So I keep my finished product in mind—a perfectly grilled burger with a toasted bun, sliced tomatoes, lettuce, pickles, onions, and a whole range of condiments—and begin.

Efficiency Goes Hand in Hand with Predictability

Horizontal and vertical slicing achieve different goals. If you're aiming for efficiency, horizontal is the way to go. That's because horizontally sliced work is divided into individual tasks that can often be shared or combined.

When you're prepping tomatoes for regular burgers, for instance, you can also prep them for the veggie burgers, Greek salad, and salsa. Preparing all the tomatoes for all the dishes in one go is faster than preparing them at different times.

Maximizing efficiency is great for predictable projects, but for the unknown and the unpredictable—which is usually how life happens, right?—it's a different story. If people show up early, and you don't have time to make the salad or salsa, prepping all the tomatoes will have been a waste of time and resources. In other words, organizing for efficiency can backfire when surprises pop up.

Many of us know this from large projects: unforeseen things happen, and already-finished work lands in the trash. Even worse, you sometimes have to keep working on tasks that are clearly doomed for the trash. Both are the unfortunate symptoms of focusing on efficiency in an unpredictable environment.

When work turns out to be worthless, this question arises: What does progress mean?

Measure Progress in Real Time

To get everything done in time for your party, you check things off as you complete them. You feel a sense of accomplishment with each crossed-off item, but if you wash and cut tomatoes for the salsa that you later omit from the menu, are you measuring real progress?

Even though it seems like it, no, you aren't. If people show up early and you don't make the salsa after all, prepping the tomatoes for that dish doesn't contribute to the *final result*: what your guests will see on the table. This is one example of how unpredictability changes what we mean by progress.

What if unpredictability doesn't come from others' time schedules but your cooking skills? When you make a dish for the first time, you're not thinking about efficiency but rather, *Will this work? Will it be a success?* You want to achieve your end goal: a tasty dish. *Effectiveness* is what you are after.

> **Optimizing for efficiency** minimizes the effort and resources needed to achieve a fixed goal.

> **Optimizing for effectiveness** maximizes the impact achieved with a fixed amount of resources.

Occasionally, I'll get the wild idea to try out a new recipe for a dinner party, and I'll just dive right in, despite not really knowing how long each step might take. Sometimes, my enthusiasm is rewarded, but more often, it invites disastrous results.

Many Italian grandmothers can make tiramisu, for instance, without a recipe, but this seemingly simple dessert is actually difficult for a first-timer. There are several key steps that, if done incorrectly, can turn it into a complete flop. If you've never made tiramisu before, the project is unpredictable—you don't know what might go wrong.

Simply knowing that you've already soaked your biscuits in espresso doesn't help you understand what the final dish will taste like; neither does whipping up the mascarpone cheese with the sugar and egg yolks. At some point, you may feel like you're 80 percent done, but these individual steps are not true markers of your progress.

It is only *after* you've assembled *the entire dessert* that you realize the coffee must've been too hot, because the biscuits are disintegrating and turning to mush. By the time you notice, your tiramisu is ruined. Now you have to start all over.

That 80 percent doneness you thought you'd achieved? Now you're at 0 percent.

When doing something for the first time, the only way to know if you've made progress or not is when it's completely done. You can't rely on individual steps.

So how can you know that you are making progress and not just preparing a soon-to-be-thrown-away tiramisu? You can make a reduced version of the dessert, which you can use to judge the taste of the mascarpone, determine how much of it needs to be added to the dish, figure out how long to submerge the biscuits into the coffee, and make adjustments if needed. This prototype will either show you that you are on the right track or uncover mistakes you are making. It can help you measure progress earlier.

Here we feel the limits of this dinner metaphor. Your guests might still be happy if you present them with soggy tiramisu, but clients won't be so understanding.

When Work Gets Complicated

It's one thing to imagine how well vertical slicing works if you're throwing a dinner party. You can see right away how seamlessly it helps with delegating work, reducing scope, and seeing the finished product in advance, especially when unpredictability is a factor (and it almost always is).

But how does vertical slicing translate to the real world? What are the benefits of adopting vertical slicing techniques in the workplace? And how can you learn to use them yourself?

In the following chapters, we'll begin to explore the different ways vertical slicing can reshape what work looks like. Then we'll look at how this shift can supercharge productivity despite unpredictability, allowing you to fast-track even the most sluggish projects.

Three Different Organizations, All with a Similar Problem

Vertical slicing techniques, some of which we've just illustrated with a simple dinner party, can be adapted by any organization. Whether it's at a government, commercial, or nonprofit organization, the work behind any process, product, or service can be sliced vertically.

To demonstrate how vertical slicing plays out in different business models, I've used three examples throughout the book. Even though these fictional organizations vary in terms of size, what they do, and the challenges they face, there are similarities between them.

As you read about Susan at Bread & More, Jenny at the Department of Emergency Support and Housing, and Thomas at Grow Your Nonprofit, try to imagine yourself in their positions. What would you do? What steps might you take to solve similar problems?

Meet Susan

Bread & More is a company-owned, national bakery chain with five hundred stores and five thousand employees. It's best known for its dozens of types of fresh-baked bread, but it also serves a variety of pastries.

Lately, the company's croissant sales have been lagging nationwide. Susan, the quality control manager at company headquarters, is puzzled. For most bakeries, croissants are a key driver of revenue, and at one point, they were one of Bread & More's top sellers. Yet now, customer reviews imply that the quality of the company's croissants has gone down.

At Bread & More, the croissants are assembled in a central commissary, frozen in their unbaked state, then shipped to all of its locations. At each store, they're baked every morning so they can be served warm. Susan needs to find out why the quality of the once-popular French pastry is suddenly tanking and what she can do to turn it around, fast.

Susan has worked on similar projects before. Each started with long phases for analysis, planning, and implementation, but critical problems often became evident only when the project was rolled out, and by then, it was far too late to make any changes. This time she will organize things another way, but how?

Meet Jenny

Jenny oversees the Department of Emergency Support and Housing, a three hundred–employee state government organization that provides emergency housing, food, and medicine for people in need, such as the homeless and refugees. Its services are implemented in various locations around her state.

From intake to moving people into their new, furnished quarters, it's a massive operation with many moving parts. And because it's a state organization, there are built-in requirements for accountability: accurate recordkeeping of the people being assisted, the processes designed to help them, and those who are implementing the processes.

As team leader, Jenny oversees the acquisition and management of accommodations with a team of nine: an architect, attorney, facility manager, and contract negotiator, among others. She's been in charge of the team for some time, and normally she delegates tasks and then gathers the results, like a teacher picking up everyone's homework at the end of class. It's time-consuming, but it's how she's been able to meet all of the requirements and government protocols.

Recently, two emergencies cropped up at the same time. A war in a neighboring country meant a sudden flood of refugees and an economic downturn in her own country, which together caused an increase in the homeless population in her state. With thousands of people suddenly needing help, Jenny is overloaded. She is unable to serve everyone because the processes that are in place for acquiring and equipping new accommodations aren't set up to adapt quickly to this new situation.

Jenny knows from experience that any plan made inside her organization has to be completely revised once it becomes reality, even though it takes a significant amount of time to create and decide on a plan in the first place. What can she do differently, she wonders, to speed up the process so her organization can respond as effectively as it needs to?

Meet Thomas

Grow Your Nonprofit is a nonprofit with a staff of twenty-five that helps other small nonprofits scale up once they've had initial success. They do this by providing educational resources and mentorship.

Although the staff at Grow Your Nonprofit ebbs and flows according to each year's annual budget, Thomas, a project manager, has been in place for several years. Like everyone at Grow Your Nonprofit, he is highly motivated and purpose driven. No one on his team knows the organization's internal processes like he does.

Like any nonprofit, various unpredictable factors may impact Grow Your Nonprofit's work: shifting societal and political changes, what volunteers are most passionate about, what subsidies nonprofits can apply for, etc. Because Thomas is one of the most experienced people on the staff, he usually is the one to notice the need for change and make necessary adjustments. He then assigns tasks to other team members and frequently checks their work.

Thomas is currently in the planning stages of

launching a new campaign, a call for applications for small nonprofits that would benefit from his organization's mentoring services. He has a team of six people working underneath him, but he's tired of coordinating their every move. He wants this project to be different but isn't sure where to begin.

As you can see, these three stories are all different, but Susan, Jenny, and Thomas face similar challenges. They're all working within a rigid, traditional system that isn't giving them the options that they need to address the unpredictability they face. Each one of them feels stuck in their roles. Over the next several chapters, we'll check in with them and see how their stories change as they learn to solve problems through vertical slicing.

▶ Work can be broken down, or "sliced," two different ways: horizontally and vertically. How you slice work will impact how you assign and check work, who takes ownership of the work, and your ability to identify surprises and adapt accordingly.

▶ Horizontal slices are the actions, steps, or tasks that must be done to create a specific result. They're best used for predictable projects that require efficiency, and they can be given to less-experienced individuals.

▶ Vertical slices are the best option when unpredictability is a factor. They give an overview, allowing you to manage scope and measure progress. They can be assigned to capable individuals and teams.

2

What's Self-Organization, Anyway?

When it comes to organizing traffic flow, there are two different systems. One's the traditional traffic light, which tells people when to stop and go; it needs energy and electricity, and it sometimes requires a long wait at a red light, even when there's no traffic at all.

Operating traffic lights can get complicated. Adjustments need to be made for different intersections, for traffic flowing in different directions and different times of day or even times of year. What seems like an automatic system requires constant oversight, and that's when everything's working just as it should—without some unforeseen event occurring, like an electricity outage.

Then there's the roundabout, a circular system with roads flowing in and out of it. Cars enter, yield to other cars, then make their exit. It's a system that requires no energy, just some rules, and it works. It outshines the traffic-light system most where traffic is unpredictable.

This is what self-organization looks like. It's simple and effective, and there's a built-in shared responsibility for the outcome. In this case, everyone who drives in and out of the roundabout partly owns its success.

The same self-organization techniques used in a roundabout can also work in a business. And when teams work together, people become empowered. They become owners of the result.

Unlock the Power of Self-Organization

Let's look at a common example of how self-organization is circumvented.

A manager has just been promoted from his previous role as the company's top sales person. In his old position, because the company was new and the staff was small, he did it all: cold calls, client communication, contract writing, and closing.

Since he started, the company's doubled in size, and his job requirements have changed. He now manages a department of new hires who are tasked with carrying out what he used to do. Because he is the only one who can see the big picture—how the whole transaction needs to play out and in what timeline—he meticulously oversees it all.

Because the new hires don't have the years of experience that their manager does, he wants to help them learn the ropes. He tries to teach them how to do things by parsing out small and specific jobs for them to complete, and after that, he sometimes gives them tasks with more responsibility. It's not that he doesn't trust them to do a good job; he is just trying *to help*. But he constantly hovers over them and course-corrects before things get too far offtrack.

Soon, the manager realizes that all of his well-intentioned guidance seems to have been wasted. As qualified as each of his team members is, no one seems to be able to think or act on their own; instead, they're always waiting to be given the next task and deadline. He realizes that he isn't delegating; he is babysitting. And it's exhausting.

Many managers fall into this *micromanagement trap*. When work is sliced horizontally, they can't avoid it. That's because this way of working is designed to keep people in their assigned roles, doing only the job that they've been given and nothing more. What's worse is that when there's a work overload, these managers often add more people, which means that they have more people to oversee.

In contrast, when vertically sliced work is handed over to teams, they intuitively *self-organize* and make decisions on their own—like drivers going in and out of a roundabout. Instead of waiting for tasks to be handed down by their superiors, they work independently or collaborate with others while keeping the end goal in mind.

Vertically sliced work saves time, produces better and faster results, and shifts all of the coordination, responsibility, and ownership away from you and onto your team members.

People Talk Among Themselves and Make Quick Decisions

Under the right conditions, self-organization can occur spontaneously among people who've never met. This is always motivating and empowering.

Here is something I've experienced over and over again. At large conferences, hundreds of attendees are asked to move all of the tables to the right side of the room and all of the chairs to the left so that they can interact more easily. At once, everyone looks at each other before calmly standing up. The stronger people begin picking up the tables and carrying them to one side, while the others take a chair or two and move them to the other side. If needed, queues form, and people help each other.

In less than two minutes, the whole thing is done because everyone *self-organized*. Each individual thought about how they could contribute best to the end result. Was there a chair in front of them, or had it already been taken by their neighbor? If so, should they help carry a table instead?

No one needs to tell them how to execute this project. They talk to each other. They sort it out. They act. Through simultaneous communication and decision-making, people coordinate among themselves. They take ownership.

Imagine the coordination it would take if you were a manager who had to organize this chair-and-table-moving process. How many different sets of directions would you have to give? How complicated might it be? How would you distribute all of this information to them in a timely manner, and how would you track that they received it and what the results were? Think of all this management overhead.

Luckily, all of this micromanaging isn't needed when people self-organize. But it also isn't enough just to tell people to self-organize and leave them to it. If a speaker said, "Make sure the room is free of obstacles," that'd be far too vague. Instead of collaborating, people would spend time trying to figure out what the obstacles were and where to put them. They'd need to agree on where to put the chairs and tables, and with hundreds of people, making a decision might take a long time. Self-organization often fails in organizations due to a lack of clarity.

As a leader, you've got to create the conditions for self-organization to happen. Clearly defining the final result, the vertical slices of work, plays a central role in this.

The End's Always in Sight

In his international bestseller, *The 7 Habits of Highly Effective People*, author Stephen R. Covey says to "Begin with the end in mind." He explains that when you do this, you create your desired outcome twice: first, in your imagination, and second, in the real world.[1]

---

1   Stephen R. Covey, *The 7 Habits of Highly Effective People* (New York: Simon & Schuster, 2013).

Fig. 4: By sharing your vision for what the end result should look like, you enable self-organization.

Having clearly described goals helps individuals, but it's even more critical for teams at work. Each member needs to have the same result in mind.

That's why self-organization works so well when conference attendees are asked to move tables and chairs: each person is acting autonomously, yet they have a clear sense of what their contribution to the whole should be. Their actions may be different, but they are all working together harmoniously to achieve the same end goal.

Giving a group a clear picture of what the results need to look like is a necessary condition for self-organization.

Why the "Why" Matters

Just having a clear picture of the final result is not enough to self-organize effectively. We also need to know *why* this particular result, or output, matters. What impact is it supposed to have? The answer to these questions is the outcome.

When something isn't going according to plan, knowing the outcome allows us to deal with the details of the job ourselves. For example, if there isn't enough space left on the right side of the room for a table, individuals can make their own decisions about where to put it in order to create a space where everyone can move freely.

> **The outcome** is the measure by which we'll judge our results. For instance, once everyone has moved tables and chairs, how freely can they move around the room?
>
> We need an **action** (horizontal slice) to get an **output** (vertical slice) that could lead to the **outcome** we hope to achieve.

Focusing on the *why* also increases motivation. If we feel connected with what we are doing, and if it is something that we believe is helping other people, it increases our performance and productivity.

A 2008 study found that firefighters who were intrinsically motivated to do their jobs demonstrated significantly higher persistence, performance, and productivity.[2] Similarly, another study showed fundraising callers who

---

2   Adam M. Grant, "Does Intrinsic Motivation Fuel the Prosocial Fire? Motivational Synergy in Predicting Persistence, Performance, and Productivity," *Journal of Applied Psychology* 93, no. 1 (2008): 48–58, https://doi.org/10.1037/0021-9010.93.1.48.

felt connected to their cause were able to raise more money than other callers.

These examples illustrate the link between outcome, motivation, and productivity. Without knowing the outcome, people don't develop intrinsic motivation, let alone work productively.

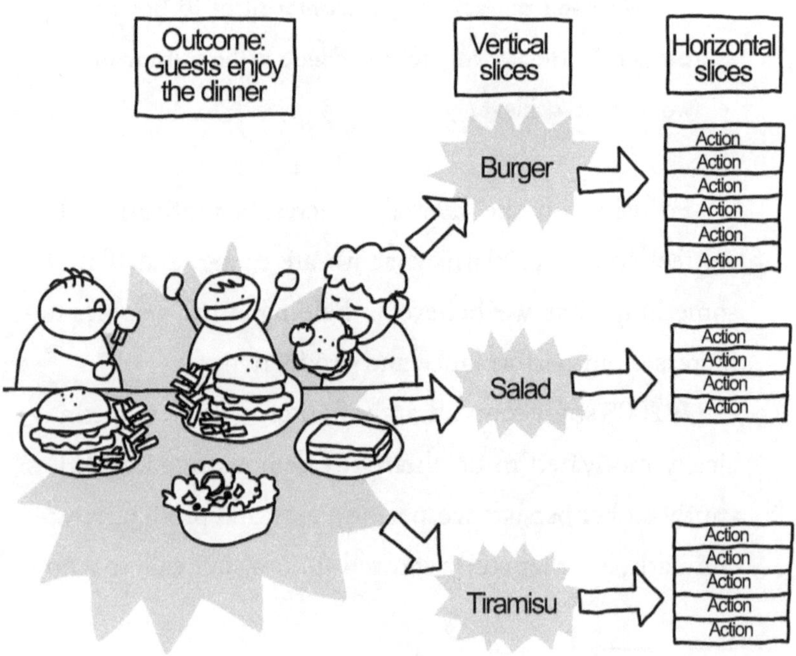

Fig. 5: Cutting tomatoes (horizontal slice) contributes to making burgers (vertical slice). Hopefully, the taste of the burgers will impress the guests (outcome).

There's a Built-In Fraud Detector

If a vertically sliced team is asked to work on a morally questionable project—such as manipulating the public or creating a product that's known to be addictive—self-organization won't be effective. Self-organization works well when we know *the why* behind it and can all rally behind with a good and clear conscience.

Because the goal of a project must be authentic in order for individuals to accept it and self-organize, team members effectively filter out whatever seems disingenuous. If something smells fishy, they may refuse to take part, sabotaging the entire process.

That's why *the why* matters—why it's critical to communicate your reasoning to your team if you'd like for them to self-organize. That's also why I like relying on self-organization so much: it's a productivity multiplier for good causes.

Sometimes Roles Can Get Squishy

Unlike traditional processes where people don't stray from their assigned roles, vertical slicing requires self-organization and collaboration across various platforms in order to be successful. Achieving one tangible result is what counts; it's not just everyone fulfilling their work obligation. But for this to happen, the understanding of roles needs to shift.

When teams are in danger of missing a project deadline, companies often bring together all the key people in one room and ask them to work as much as needed to get the project through the door in time. I've heard many different names for this—"crunch time," "code yellow," and "war zone," to name a few—but during this time, formal roles are meaningless. People just contribute whatever they can to succeed with the project.

If you've ever been in the room during crunch time, you know this is often when many of the most significant results are achieved and decisions are met. Imagine being that productive as a team without the same level of exhaustion. That's what it feels like to work on a team that practices vertical slicing.

Let's see how Jenny's team uses their expertise outside of their traditional roles to help identify solutions for the flood of refugees who'll need emergency housing in just a few weeks.

Jenny's Team Takes Ownership Together

The single women, men, children, and entire families Jenny and her team need to support come from both sides of the war. They arrive hungry and in need of medical care, and they speak different languages. Helping them would be a massive challenge even if they had months to prepare.

Jenny calls a meeting with her team members—including the architect, quality assurance manager, building inspector, facility manager, and refugee law expert—to come up with a solution. Acquiring a new building to accommodate the refugees isn't an option; the entire process usually takes six to nine months and includes research, analysis, building acquisition, and renovation. The only option, they all agree, is to expand the occupancy of some of their existing buildings to absorb these additional hundreds of people, but how?

Jenny's team begins to conceptualize together, own *the entire project* together, and imagine the whole, finished solution together. That's because, as experts in their particular fields, each team member naturally has knowledge of other disciplines. Like the facility manager, the architect has a good understanding of a room's layout and knows how many people it might hold. The law expert who normally negotiates contracts with landlords also knows about the intricacies of facility management. Because the quality assurance manager usually deals with individual cases, they also have insight into which residents will best live with others. These natural connections between team members allow for easy collaboration, while at the same time erasing some of the hard lines previously drawn around each of their roles.

Jenny asks her team to come up with a short list of risks associated with moving refugees into existing buildings. The top risk, they agree, is that existing residents will not get along with the newcomers. To test this assumption, they ask some residents to make room for ten refugees. This happens faster than they ever could have imagined, since normally, *any* action would only happen after months of work trying to get the concept approved.

After a week, they learn that different people with different living situations are either more or less open to different types of newcomers. Families easily adapt to having one more young person in their space, and elderly women easily share their spaces too. But, in some cases, new inhabitants fear for their personal safety and request that they be moved.

To quickly accommodate everyone's needs, collaboration between team members is vital. That's because they have to make decisions every day that require diverse knowledge and abilities involving resources, language support, architectural stability, and myriad laws and regulations that apply to both old and new inhabitants.

Jenny's team uses this experience to take a second vertical slice of the project the following week, this time with twenty people in a different building. By the end of the second week, she and her team formalize what they've learned and are able to come up with a strong list of recommendations derived from their real-world experience.

In the following weeks, their recommendations are applied to house even more people. Not everything works smoothly, but they are able to react when things go wrong, and they learn and adapt much faster than in their previous processes.

Note that the fluidity of roles is key to Jenny's team's success. She built a multidisciplinary team, and they spent 100 percent of their time devoted to one specific project goal. The vertically sliced way kept everyone focused on the outcome: getting the refugees safely housed.

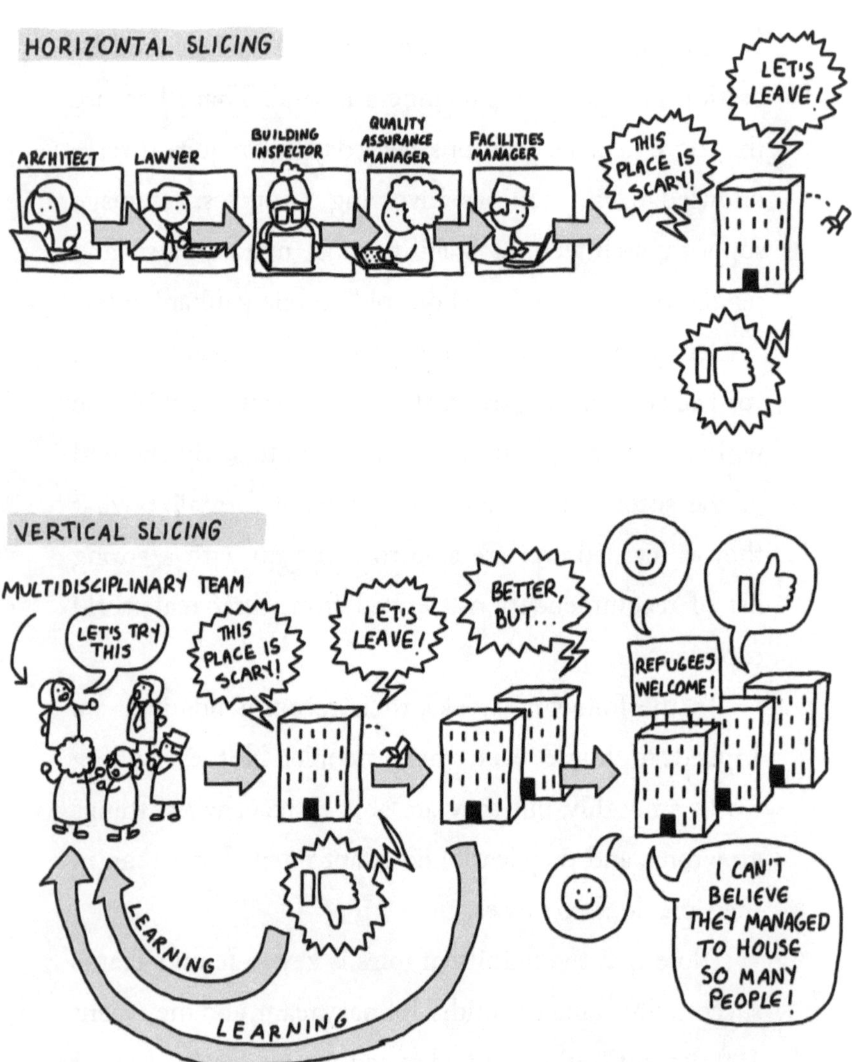

Fig. 6: Comparison of the traditional sequential process of handing over tasks from one area of expertise to the next and getting results at the very end (above) with delivering vertical slices as a multidisciplinary team and learning from one slice to the next (below).

"Help Wanted" Takes on a Different Meaning

When an organization requires the kind of collaboration that Jenny and her team adopted, the old model for hiring needs to change. No longer are individuals hired solely for one particular role, but for the skills that they bring to the company and their willingness to be part of a truly cross-functional team. They need to be open to sharing expertise and working together toward a common goal.

In other words, hiring for a team that practices vertical slicing requires a different set of expectations. A different way of working. However, you don't need to change all the human resources processes to leverage the power of cross-functional teamwork. In most organizations, there already are lots of employees who long to have more impact.

When you begin your first vertical slicing initiatives, these people will typically volunteer. Once these initiatives show positive results, they pave the way for more people in the organization to rethink their ways of working, including processes for hiring and promoting.

Why Self-Organization Works

Self-organization is powerful. It changes how people work and how they work together. And like for Jenny's team helping refugees, it can happen quickly, if certain conditions are met:

- The project is staffed with dedicated people who are able to make their own decisions on the most important matters of the project.
- The project is vertically sliced into results that contribute to a clear, motivating outcome.
- Team members frequently check whether delivering those slices is actually as valuable as they hope.

The last point—getting frequent feedback—is the next vital feature of vertically sliced work. As you'll see in the next chapter, it has the potential to improve productivity even more.

▶ Self-organization speeds up work because people simultaneously communicate and make decisions on their own.

▶ Self-organization works only when you assign vertical slices of work to capable groups and explain the reason why this work makes a difference—the outcome. When this happens, groups own the result together, and individual roles become more fluid.

▶ Hiring changes from looking for experts with specific knowledge and experience to finding individuals who can be skilled team contributors.

3

Feedback Can Fix It, and Fast

Remember our discussion about creating a smaller version of tiramisu to gather feedback on what's working and what's not before preparing the entire dessert? This approach could prevent you from serving a soggy mess to your guests and help you master the art of making this dish.

Feedback's a lot like a Swiss Army knife. It's a tool that can improve or fix almost anything, but its effectiveness depends on how the work is sliced, which determines who can give the feedback and what criteria their feedback is going to be based on.

- An outsider can provide feedback on a *vertical slice*, without understanding how it was made.

This outsider might be a customer, end user, or stakeholder.

- Only an expert, someone who knows how a particular task needs to be performed, can give feedback on the result of a *horizontal slice*.

The difference in feedback on a vertical versus horizontal slice looks like this:

- Any dinner guest can say whether they liked a burger, but typically someone who has prepared burgers before will have an informed opinion about whether the bun was properly prepared.
- A family can assess if a new home is comfortable and fits their needs, but only a skilled mason can evaluate a newly built wall.

Feedback on a vertical slice is more holistic and allows for greater creativity. For instance, you could experiment with tomato thickness and find that, contrary to the expert opinion, some people love burgers with very thick tomatoes. This permission to experiment promotes both ownership and a desire for continuous improvement of the entire result. On the other hand, feedback on horizontal slices improves the craft associated with that specific task.

In either case, the benefit of feedback is quite simple: whatever gets feedback gets improved.

How Feedback Works With Vertical Slices

Susan, our quality control manager at Bread & More, wants to unravel the mystery of why her company's croissant quality has gone flat. In the past, she's worked on projects where problems became evident only after the project was rolled out—far too late to make any changes—so she intends to tackle this mystery in a more pragmatic fashion. By slicing the project vertically.

Susan calls a meeting and invites a cross section of people to attend, all of whom are involved in the croissant-making process: a representative from the commissary where the croissants are formed, frozen, and boxed for shipment; someone from the refrigerated truck company; the company's top bakers; several store managers; and even some hourly employees. After explaining the project's goal—to determine why croissant quality has nose-dived and fix it—she asks the group to imagine what could've gotten offtrack, from the beginning of the process to the final, baked product. They identify dozens of possibilities, including the temperature of the trucks; delivery time of the frozen product; the ovens, which differ from one store to the next; and the display cases, some of which are closed and some of which are open air.

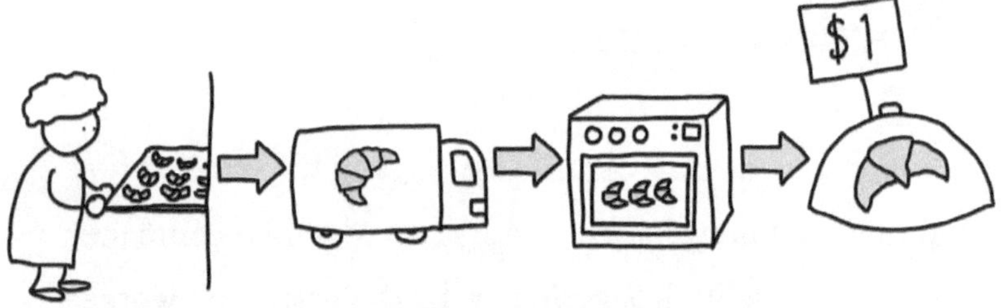

Fig. 7: Steps of a croissant: 1. formed and frozen,
2. shipped, 3. baked, and 4. put on display.

They then rank the potential issues from high to low, according to likelihood they could impact the quality of the croissants. They all agree that the most likely problem—and the costliest one—is that the ovens aren't heating evenly or at the correct temperature. After all, each branch has a different oven model; some are new, but others are several years old.

To test this hypothesis, Susan's team chooses ten locations, half of which have the highest croissant sales and half of which have the lowest. These locations use several different types of ovens, so Susan and her team can compare the quality of the croissants baked at each location and determine whether the worst croissants are at the locations with the oldest ovens. How will they know if the croissants are any good? By tearing them apart and tasting them themselves. No months-long-analysis process needed.

After two weeks, they determine the problem isn't the ovens at all. The croissants had the same amount of crispness, lightness, and flakiness at all locations because employees at each branch adapted the baking times and temperatures for their particular ovens. Who would have thought that their main assumption was incorrect, that employees would change the prescribed process to bake better pastries?

Since their first vertical slice got negative feedback, Susan and her team look at the next likely culprit and soon discover the inconsistency. The display cases—some of which are glassed in and some of which are open air—either keep the croissants crisp or quickly turn them dry.

They then replace open-air display cases with ones that are closed in five different bakeries to verify if this improves croissant quality. This second vertical slice quickly results in positive feedback from customers, which leads to a speedy approval from top management to deliver their next vertical slices: closed displays for

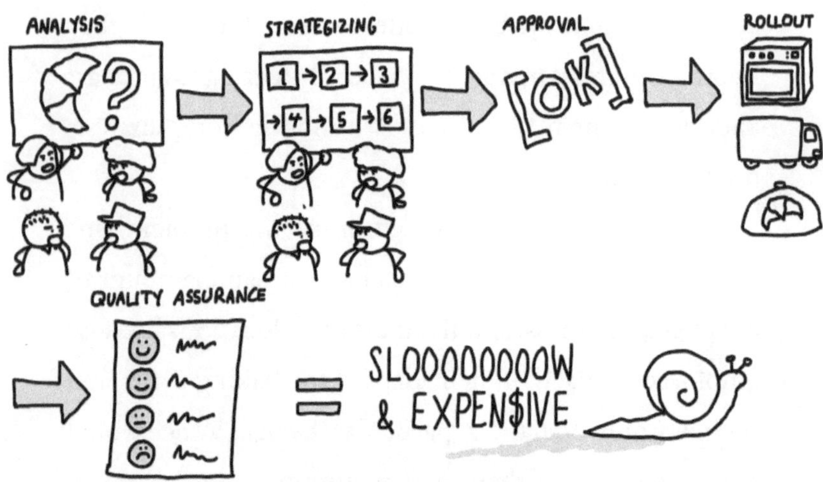

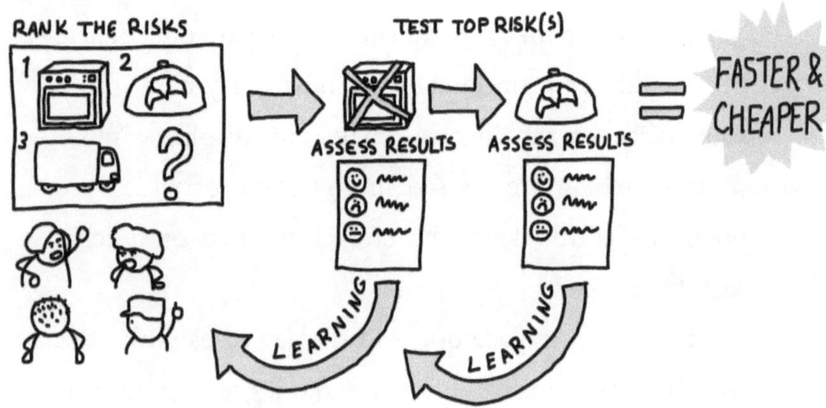

Fig. 8: Comparison of the traditional sequential process from analysis to rollout. Above: teams don't learn what works and what does not until the very end. Below: teams deliver vertical slices and learn from each slice delivered. Identifying dead ends early on saves time and money.

croissants in all branches. Even more significant, they are able to make the change right away.

By using vertical slices, Susan was able to choose the most promising path for her project, then move on when she realized ovens were not the problem. But if the ovens' results had been different, the project would've taken a different path.

This is what navigating unpredictability looks like.

Furthermore, instead of using traditional, time-consuming methods that involve endless analysis and strategizing before implementation, Susan's team identified the problem and delivered tangible results within weeks. How? By taking the project one vertical slice at a time: baking croissants in different ovens was one slice, and displaying croissants in different cases was another.

The results of each slice were clear, providing the team with actionable feedback. But this project was truly a success because the team identified potential problems together, reflected on their progress together, and was open as a group to the results—not tied to any preconceptions.

Learning from Each Other

Susan and her team determining that different ovens were not responsible for the varying quality of Bread & More's croissants is an example of *external learning*. They delivered a vertical slice, checked whether it was useful, and contributed to their outcome.

While delivering this result, Susan's team also learned how to work better together. This is particularly important, as her team consisted of people from very different professions. These differences led to some misunderstandings at the beginning, but they were all resolved over time. This improvement inside the team is an example of *internal learning*.

> **External learning** is the process of understanding which factors impact the target outcome of your project. It shows us which slices are impactful and which are not.

> **Internal learning** occurs when something within a process or project is changed or adapted. It also occurs when you and your team learn to work better together.

As I've learned from my own projects, both kinds of learning occur when we get feedback on vertical slices, and both have the potential to improve productivity. You shouldn't underestimate the boost in productivity that comes from internal learning.

Once, I was asked by a publisher to create indexes for over a thousand different educational textbooks. I hired eight people to assign page numbers to important elements, such as topics, images, and chapters, within each textbook, and to put this information in an individual file for each book. I also set up a vertical process where people, working in pairs, would review one textbook at a time, then switch, check each other's work, and give immediate feedback.

This feedback included questions like these: Should a box of verb tenses in a language book be indexed the same as a photo? If there is a blank page between chapters with an image, how should this image be indexed? Should a mathematical formula be indexed at all?

The pairs gave feedback to each other, then agreed on how to move forward. This feedback led to agreements, which helped create consistency across all of the books. This consistency in turn led to improved productivity and quality.

By sharing feedback, these teams of two improved

tremendously. Our group as a whole even tripled our performance from the first week to the sixth week of the project.

The Faster, the Better

Teams work faster when they share feedback right away. When feedback comes too late, they tend not to learn. The information doesn't stick.

Imagine learning to play the guitar and having to wait fifteen minutes to hear the sound of the strings that you strummed. How well would you learn? Fifteen seconds later is hard enough. Fifteen minutes? No way.

How quickly feedback comes plays a vital role in learning. With immediate feedback, we can still remember our decisions and identify what we need to change in order to improve.

Research backs this up. In his book, *Thinking, Fast and Slow*, author Daniel Kahneman writes about how significant—and potentially lifesaving—instantaneous feedback can be. He gives an example comparing how quickly anesthesiologists and radiologists receive feedback.[3]

---

3   Daniel Kahneman, *Thinking, Fast and Slow* (New York: Farrar, Straus and Giroux, 2013).

Kahneman says that health monitoring tells anesthesiologists within minutes of their giving a patient a drug if their heartbeat is slowing too much or if their blood pressure jumps. This way, they can quickly get better at their job. In contrast, radiologists may not know how accurate their diagnoses are for months or even years because they're only looking at X-rays, which are just one component of a patient's medical workup. This delayed feedback makes it much harder for radiologists to improve their skills.

In organizations, there are often meetings that highlight *lessons learned* several months after a project is complete. But it's a lot like the radiologists and the scans. To learn from an X-ray, or in business, a project, the feedback has to be immediate. The speed makes all the difference.

This is where vertical slicing plays a key role. If the next vertical slice—something a stakeholder can give feedback on—takes months to complete, you'll have to wait months to learn and adapt. But if you manage to divide your projects into vertical slices that can be accomplished in a week or two, your learning—and in turn, your projects—will start to accelerate.

Humans Are Hardwired to Adapt

Not that long ago, technology was a vague, out-of-reach concept to most of us. Biologically, we're not that different from our hunter-gatherer ancestors, and yet today, almost everyone has a smartphone and can adapt to new operating systems with ease.

Just as we adapt to rapidly changing technology, we adapt to changes in every other aspect of our lives. When your favorite restaurant closes or you move to a new place, it may take a little time to adjust, but eventually, you embrace the new situation and find benefits instead of only downsides.

As humans, we're all about cognitive adaptability, and feedback's a powerful catalyst for that process. You receive feedback any time you notice that something is different from what you expected, and you change and grow as a result. You get better at whatever you're doing, whether that's baking croissants or playing guitar. Feedback is essential because without it, no learning can occur.

Focus on the Whole

Because we adapt only in response to feedback, what we pay attention to matters. That's why *how our work is sliced* makes a big difference in what we learn.

In an environment where we receive feedback only on how well a particular activity was done, we improve the skill related only to that activity. In contrast, in an environment where we receive feedback on projects as a whole, we naturally learn and adapt in a variety of areas. This is why vertically slicing work is key to helping individuals and teams grow holistically—not just as specialists.

Productivity tripled with my textbook project because the feedback was given on how to work better in order to serve *the end result*, which in this case was the delivery of a consistent and complete index for all the textbooks. Because the team members weren't limited in their roles, and had the end goal of *one complete book* always in mind, they were able to adapt and work within a system that required more from them instead of less.

This concept may sound counterintuitive if you believe that specialized work increases productivity. However, if you enable people to get feedback, focus on the whole project, and *do more*, most will rise to the challenge. They'll work faster, and the end result will be greatly improved.

Feedback is Just One Tool

Setting up a vertical system where feedback is a built-in part of the process allows individuals and teams to identify potential problems early on and work strategically to find solutions. You won't do away with unpredictability, but you'll have better tools to deal with it when it comes along.

How do you know if a project's predictable or unpredictable? In the next chapter, you'll find out where unpredictability comes from, how to identify it, and how to manage it.

- ▶ What gets feedback gets improved. Feedback on horizontal slices (steps) leads to improvement in skills only. Feedback on vertical slices (results) enables people to learn and adapt across a whole project.

- ▶ Both external and internal learning contribute to significant increases in productivity.

- ▶ Only fast and frequent feedback leads to learning and improvement.

- ▶ Slicing a project in small, vertical slices is the key to getting fast feedback on the project as a whole—and being able to navigate unpredictability.

4

Unpredictability's Predictable Nature

Not every unknown is unpredictable.

Sometimes, a problem is merely complicated.

If you invest enough time and energy into understanding and analyzing a complicated problem, the unknown can become known. You know how it will behave, and you know what to expect from it.

For example, let's say that your car has broken down and you don't know how to fix it. That's a big unknown, but a predictable one. Your car will not run away from you (unless you forget to set the brakes), and it won't suddenly change into an airplane or a boat. It's a complicated problem, but you have all the time in the world to take the car apart, understand the issue, and learn how to fix it. You can also just go to an expert—such as a car mechanic—who can fix the problem for you.

Of course, not all problems in life—and especially in work—are as predictable as fixing a car. Sometimes, no matter how much time or expertise you invest in understanding a problem, you can't predict what will actually fix it.

Sometimes problems are unpredictable because they change faster than you can analyze them. For instance, don't even try to get your head around the internal processes of a one-month-old startup because they're constantly evolving.

Other times, trying to analyze a problem changes the problem itself. For instance, it's often difficult to figure out whether people will buy a product you've come up with in advance simply by asking them about it. Why? Because people generally care about protecting the feelings of the person asking them the question. This renders their reply useless.

Fortunately, there is good news: just because a problem is unpredictable doesn't mean it's unsolvable. In fact, unpredictability often arises in predictable ways.

In this chapter, we'll look at some main sources of unpredictability to get a better understanding of where to expect it. Then, we'll look at how unpredictability changes the nature of work. Finally, we'll discuss how to deliver the message that your project is unpredictable and how to set up a work environment that quickly recognizes when unpredictability strikes and adapts accordingly.

Where Does Unpredictability Come From?

If it seems like unpredictability is everywhere, you're not wrong. It is. Unpredictability comes from a variety of sources, and in the world we live in today, it's growing— and at an unpredictable pace.

There are four key areas of unpredictability:

- Humans
- Competition
- Technological development
- Outside factors

Let's begin by talking about the human element.

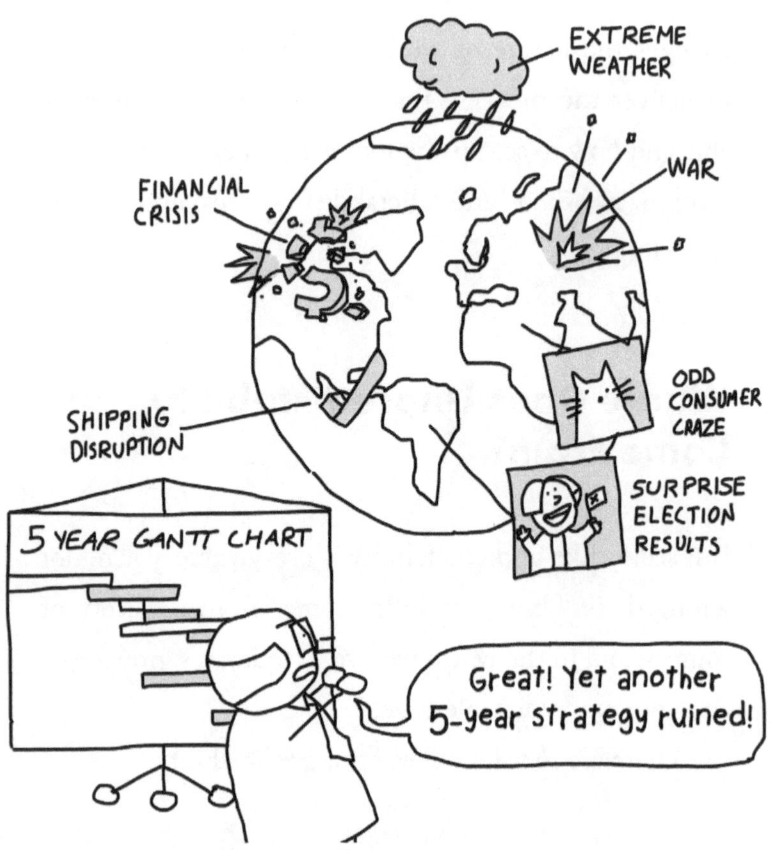

Fig. 9: A leader expecting a five-year plan
to work out in the modern world.

The Human Element

Any kind of work where humans are involved inher-
ently has high levels of unpredictability. We often don't
know how we'll behave ourselves, and when we work

with other people, it gets even messier. How we behave is governed by the relationships and agreements we have with one other, which might not be clearly expressed. This is why introducing new procedures within organizations is always unpredictable: it's impossible to foresee how each employee will react.

When Jenny at the Department of Emergency Support and Housing wanted to implement her team's plan to house ten new refugees in an existing building, she knew that simply raising the occupancy requirements wouldn't solve the problem. The refugees from one country might not get along with those from another, so they couldn't be housed together. Likewise, the existing residents might not want to share their space with strangers and might suddenly come up with a (cough, cough) grave, communicable illness in order to keep their living space as is.

Whenever you implement changes in a human system, whether increasing the density in government-provided housing or updating a process within an organization, the results will be unpredictable.

Competition Creates Unpredictability

Watching sports is so popular because competition is filled with unpredictability. You might think that you have a good idea about who's going to win a football game, for instance, but you really don't know. A team's key player could get knocked out in the first quarter, ruining their chances. Or there might be an upset because the underdog adapted so well to the other team's strategy. Anything can happen—that's what keeps us hooked.

Competition in business works the same way, and globalization has made the playing field even more intense. Unless you're targeting a niche, hyperlocal market, you're no longer competing against a few similar businesses; you're now going head-to-head with the entire world. There could be any number of people who are adapting to what you do and offering the same goods and services—often at a better value.

The Accelerating Speed of Technology

Not that long ago, computers used dial-up modems that beeped and made funny sounds, and mobile phones were the size of bricks. Today, pages load in fractions of a second—on our computers *and* our phones. It's been a wild ride, and that's just in the last fifteen years. In fact, as I'm writing this book, I'm wondering whether the next generation of artificial intelligence apps could write it better than me.

Changes in technology lead to unpredictability in work in two ways:

- Technology changes the products and services we consume, so there's a need to constantly upgrade.
- Technology changes the way products and services are produced and delivered, so employees constantly need to acquire new skills.

In 1965, Gordon Moore, a cofounder of Intel, predicted that the density of transistors, the smallest computing units in a computer, would double approximately every two years. As the result of numerous technological advances, from 1975 to 2020, his forecast proved to be correct. This prediction is now known as Moore's law.

Significant technological changes are also occurring weekly in the fields of biology and medicine. For example, the cost of sequencing human DNA has been exponentially decreasing in the last twenty years, which has allowed for individualized treatments for cancer, among other diseases.

These kinds of developments parallel those in many different technological fields, though they're often unknown to the public until a large breakthrough occurs.

What's next is anyone's guess, because technology doesn't evolve in a linear way. It changes quickly, and we can't predict *how* it might change. But whatever's next is coming too fast to predict, let alone analyze.

Outside Factors

Another source of unpredictability is outside factors, like a third-party company that's linked to your business. Perhaps they provide you with the critical elements needed to make your product, or perhaps they deliver your final product. The more vital your partner's role is, the more havoc it can create if a sudden change occurs that affects them.

Bread & More, for instance, wouldn't be able to make any of its products without its flour supplier, so imagine the ripple effect if a wheat farmer's crops were decimated by war or a drought, two unpredictable events. Without wheat, flour can't be made, and without flour, Bread & More can't bake bread.

That's a dramatic example, but smaller, unexpected changes can cause problems too. The employees of the delivery company could go on strike, causing delays. Refrigerated trucks might break down, losing all of the frozen croissants that were on their way to stores. An unexpected winter storm could make roads impassable for days.

Think about the last time your computer crashed out of the blue. Or when your electricity went out for a day due to a storm or construction in your area. Unpredictable outside forces, beyond your control, have a real impact on your ability to get your work done.

Unpredictability is just about everywhere you look. If humans are involved, there's unpredictability. Competition, even more so. Technology and its accelerated speed of change, far too fast to be analyzed for future predictions to be made. Outside factors, whoever or whatever they may be.

Now that we've examined four different sources of unpredictability, let's take a closer look at two main aspects of working with unpredictability: (1) dealing with unpredictability is knowledge work, and (2) knowledge work is invisible.

Unpredictability Requires Knowledge Work

Let's say you go to IKEA and buy two identical boxes of shelves that you'll need to assemble once you get home. After you open the box and read the instructions, you begin assembling the first shelf. The first shelf takes some de-assembling along the way, some restarts; it takes an hour or two, maybe more. But then you begin to assemble the second one, which is exactly like the first. How long do you imagine this one will take to put together?

If you're like me, it will probably take half the time that it took to build the first one—or if you're having a really good day, even less. Why? Because the second time, you don't have to read the instructions again; you don't have to find out what tools to use or where to put all the parts before assembling them. When you made mistakes and corrected them the first time, you learned. Now you understand how to build the shelves the way you're supposed to.

That's how *knowledge work* works. When building the first shelf, you did both physical and knowledge work, but building the second shelf requires physical work only. If you wanted to, you could sit on your living room floor and make IKEA shelves all day long; it would simply be *physical work*, like the work that the professional assemblers do.

The same idea applies in many business situations. Let's say you've got to make an important slide-deck presentation, one that could determine your career path for the next few years. You invest several weeks in doing research, putting together your speech, and coming up with charts and graphs to illustrate your points. You even ask colleagues for feedback to improve how you communicate your message.

Then, a day before your presentation, your computer crashes. You don't have a backup, so you lose the whole presentation. But as daunting as it initially seems to reconstruct your slides, it takes only a few hours.

That's because knowledge work comprised over 90 percent of the total time you invested in your first presentation. Likewise, I believe that for many professionals today, knowledge work constitutes much more than half of the time they invest in their jobs.

> **Knowledge work** is about *creating knowledge and understanding* in order for something physical or technical to be executed.

The more unpredictable your work is, the more knowledge work dominates over other kinds of work. Once you achieve success in an unpredictable situation, repeating that success takes much less effort than you originally put in.

However, knowledge work has one big disadvantage—it's invisible. Its results are in our brains. So how do you know your colleague is doing worthy knowledge work and not just dreaming about their next holiday?

This is different from a mason who builds a wall. There, you can see and assess visible progress, but you can't know whether someone is having a productive day of knowledge work or not. And the larger your project, the more knowledge work is going on behind the scenes.

As time passes, you won't know if progress is being made unless you invest in making knowledge work tangible. You can do this by getting feedback on a vertical slice of a project, which creates points of visibility. This allows you to see progress.

Three Ingredients for Managing Unpredictable Projects

How do you manage a project when you know there may be surprises that will emerge only once you've finished the work? You finish a small part of it as early as you can, see what emerges, and repeat.

You may find yourself managing an unpredictable situation well every day—behind the wheel of a car. No matter how many years of driving experience you have, you can never predict what lane of the highway you'll be driving in or at what speed. You can never predict what other drivers will do or if there will be a traffic jam, an accident, or construction on the road. You often can't even predict whether it will rain, causing the roads to be slick and dangerous. You never really know.

The three ingredients for managing unpredictability, which you use intuitively when you drive a car, are transparency, inspection, and adaptation.[4] We'll discuss each of these in turn now.

---

4   Scrum Guides, "The 2020 Scrum Guide," 2020, https://scrumguides.org/scrum-guide.html. These are also the three empirical pillars of Scrum.

Transparency

A car is optimized for transparency. With a windshield, windows, and mirrors, drivers can view what's behind and on both sides of them at a glance, without needing to turn around. In addition, dashboards relay a car's condition.

In organizations, transparency refers to the visibility of a project's overall progress, which can be achieved via feedback loops and built-in checks on vertical slices of a project. Without such transparency, it would be difficult to notice the project going offtrack.

Inspection

Transparency enables the second ingredient: inspection. Inspection means investing time and resources in continuously checking a situation.

While driving, we need to take the time to look at the road, to see what's in front of us, and to discern what challenges we might face. In organizations, we need to set aside time and resources to check projects' overall progress.

Adaptation

When they work properly, both transparency and inspection show us when something is going wrong. And when something is wrong, we need the third ingredient: adaptation. This simply means that we have the means to adapt, that adjustments can be made in order to achieve overall success.

When driving, if a box falls off the back of a truck and lands in front of us, or if an animal suddenly appears in our way, we may need to react and change course. Fortunately, we have the means to adapt. We can use the brakes. Steer ourselves out of harm's way. Use the horn.

Fig. 10: Transparency, inspection, and adaptation in action while driving a car.

When managing work, adaptation means adjusting what you plan to work on in the future. Adding new items to your plan, removing obsolete ones, or changing how you thought something should be done.

The more unpredictability an organization faces, the more its management needs to invest in means for transparency, inspection, and adaptation. It's not easy, and often these three necessary ingredients are simply neglected. But when organizations ignore this need, it's much like driving a car with a muddy windshield (zero transparency) while texting instead of looking at the road (lack of inspection), and without access to the steering wheel or the brakes (no means for adaptation).

How to Communicate Unpredictability? Very Carefully

Unpredictability is inevitable, yet it often causes anxiety. When surprises pop up, it may look like you don't have your process or your teams under control, and you don't want to look incompetent. Clients don't want to hear about any issues either, for fear of their requests becoming more expensive.

Unpredictability plays right into our insecurities, but it doesn't have to. It's all in how the message is delivered.

There are several ways to talk about unpredictability

without even mentioning the word. The key to keeping resistance low and constructiveness high is focusing on the impact of your project—not on the unpredictable elements. The impact is what everyone is interested in, anyway. It's also the best way to align different stakeholders.

I'll describe how to set up your project in Chapter 8, but for now, I will suggest some short, concrete ways to lead such conversations. These are particularly useful if you want to sensitize other people to taking unpredictability head-on.

First, when you begin discussing your project with stakeholders, ask them to imagine two different scenarios:

- The project is a success, beyond your greatest expectations. What will be different when it's completed?
- Now imagine this project failed in every possible way. What are all the things that went wrong?

Through these two scenarios, you can help them see areas where unpredictability may occur. Next, ask: What intermediary results—vertical slices—can help you reduce the greatest risks or ensure some of the most important hopes will be delivered?

- If you've done a similar project, you might make a list of all of its pluses and minuses. What worked well and what didn't? Thinking about vertical slices in a similar project will help you to identify unpredictable factors and risks in the current project earlier. You also may find some instances when a result was checked early on, which helped steer the project in the right direction.

- A more direct method is to map out all of the unknowns connected to a project. This works well if you are working with a larger group of people and can ask them to visualize all the things they don't yet know about the project that are important for its success. You can even let everyone present their visualizations to the group and make a list of all the unknowns uncovered this way.

Through these practices, you acknowledge to the stakeholders that you're managing a project with a number of risks. You then assure them that you'll put in place measures to ensure timely feedback, including these:

- Transparency about results
- Time and resources for inspection
- The means to adapt the project

Unpredictability can't be avoided, and it exists in most jobs. Yet with feedback, you can recognize it, communicate it to others, and manage it.

But feedback isn't easy for either the giver or the receiver. Difficult emotions can arise on both sides. Find out why this happens in the next chapter, along with some tips on how to best deliver feedback.

▶ Most projects have a substantial amount of unpredictability within them. This unpredictability comes from human dynamics, competition, fast-changing technology, and outside factors like reliance on business partners.

▶ Dealing with unpredictability is knowledge work. Knowledge work is invisible.

▶ Three ingredients are required to successfully manage unpredictable projects: high transparency on results, the ability to continuously inspect these results, and the ability to adapt as needed.

▶ There are strategies to help you communicate and identify unpredictable areas of your project without triggering anxiety.

5

Manage Emotional Resistance to Feedback

In projects with lots of unpredictability, failure is unavoidable. The best thing we can do is ask ourselves what we can learn from it, then move on. However, effectively giving and receiving critical feedback can be emotionally tricky. It can feel a lot like criticism and judgment, taking us back to grade school report cards and teachers' red notes.

It's easy to take feedback personally. *We did something wrong. We're not good enough. We should've done better. Our project failed.* We *failed.* Being on the receiving end of feedback can really hurt.

Feedback often brings up insecurities and negative emotions, such as these:

- Feeling inadequate. *I'm such an idiot.*
- Feeling rejected. *I'll lose my job.*
- Feeling unappreciated. *Don't they see how hard I'm working?*

Giving feedback is risky too:

- It can damage relationships.
- The receiver might get defensive, countering with their own arguments and creating a negative spiral.
- If the feedback is factually wrong, we might have to apologize.

No one wants to deliver bad news to a coworker, even if it's not intended to sting, which is why many organizations struggle with giving feedback. But avoiding feedback altogether can hamstring the process of working with unpredictability.

To ensure feedback is shared, organizations can do the following:

- Employ vertical slicing
- Invest in feedback infrastructure
- Learn how to effectively give and receive feedback
- Trust the process

We'll discuss each of these strategies in turn.

Employ Vertical Slicing

Vertical slicing can shift how feedback is viewed within organizations, on both the giving and receiving ends. It can reduce the risk of people taking feedback personally and instead allow them to hear what's constructive and tune out the rest.

Here's how. When teams employ vertical slicing, delivering small results that can be evaluated by stakeholders instead of the whole project, they realize the feedback given is on the work itself—not on them personally. If one small piece fails, it doesn't have the same impact as if the whole project fails, which makes the feedback easier to receive.

Slicing the project into small pieces also allows for feedback to be given more frequently, which makes people more comfortable with giving and receiving it.

When people get used to failure simply being information, they realize that it's not always that big of a deal.

Invest in Feedback Infrastructure

When an organization recognizes the value of frequent
feedback, managers are faced with the challenge of
determining how to obtain it. There's often no access
to stakeholders, and individuals may not know how to
solicit and receive feedback effectively. Regardless of the
specifics, establishing feedback infrastructure requires
both creativity and financial investment.

Here are some common processes organizations put
in place:

1. Scheduling a biweekly meeting when the people
   who do the work assess how impactful their
   work actually was
2. Assembling a group of users, people who benefit
   from what you do, who are willing to provide
   frequent and confidential feedback
3. Collecting customer satisfaction data, as often as
   weekly, using surveys

4. Closely integrating the support department with the rest of the organization to facilitate better communication and feedback exchange

5. Renegotiating contracts with clients to require regular feedback

You may also have to get creative with establishing your feedback infrastructure. For instance, a client of mine, a niche hardware manufacturer, was once in the process of remaking their legacy product and needed to get feedback on the changes. Yet they didn't want word to get out because the market was so small and the competition so fierce. If a rival company heard about the project in advance, they could compromise the product relaunch by spreading rumors or false information.

In order to keep the project under wraps, this company hired someone who recently retired from a customer's company, where they used the product daily, to test the new version and give feedback. It was an out-of-the-box solution to assemble what was basically a focus group of one, but it worked. When organizations work under conditions of tremendous unpredictability and high stakes like this one, investing in feedback infrastructure via an outside source is a necessity.

Learn How to Effectively Give and Receive Feedback

In my experience, once feedback infrastructure is in place, everyone involved still needs to learn how to deal with the emotional aspect of giving and receiving feedback. There are dozens of books that focus solely on this topic, but I will share only the three methods that I've had the most success with.

The Perfection Game

The simplest feedback technique I know of is one developed by Jim and Michele McCarthy, called "The Perfection Game."[5] It's quite straightforward:

1. You ask for feedback about a specific thing from someone. It might be about how you performed or something you created.
2. They start by rating the performance or creation overall, from one to ten.

---

5   For more details please check The Core Protocols at https:// thecoreprotocols.org/.

3. They list everything they liked about it in detail.

4. They cite improvements that need to be made for it to become a ten.

Note: If the feedback-giver can't say how to make the performance or creation better, they must give it a ten.

Ritual Dissent

With most organizations, I teach a method developed by Dave Snowden called "Ritual Dissent." It helps take the ego out of the feedback process, as well as sparks insight into the value of negative feedback.

Here's how it works. First, you explain to a small group what you'd like to receive feedback on, such as your project plan or business idea. Their assignment: to imagine that it's a terrible and even dangerous idea for their company, talk to each other, find as many weak points as they can, and simply destroy it.

Fig. 11: With Ritual Dissent, you invite others to destroy your idea, make notes on what criticism sticks, and use that criticism to improve.

You keep your back to them so that they don't see your face and don't talk to you. Then you simply eavesdrop on their conversation, noting all the relevant points.

In this scenario, because people can't see your face, they feel free to say whatever they want. Meanwhile, because they're talking to each other rather than directly to you, you can really hear and understand what they're saying—and not get entangled in justifications.

When there are high levels of unpredictability, it's easy to overlook something important. But when you invite different perspectives, you increase your chances of uncovering all possible negative points.

Snowden's process helps groups avoid quickly coming to an agreement with too little discussion. It also allows for criticism within a group to surface and makes feedback easy to be heard and accepted. Once successfully implemented and practiced, it's a useful technique that can help to change an organization's culture from feedback-avoiding to feedback-seeking.

> **Works great for:** Soliciting feedback from several people at once. Best used on results of work, new concepts, and plans.

Clean Feedback

When it comes to addressing someone's behavior, I use and teach a technique called "Clean Feedback" developed by Caitlin Walker. There are many aspects to Walker's technique, but basically, the feedback-giver shares three parts of their feedback:

1. Evidence: what they heard, observed, or perceived
2. Inference: how they interpreted it and what they are now assuming

3. Impact: what the effect is now

Here's something the feedback-giver might say in an email without using the Clean Feedback method: "Are you trying to have me walk right into a trap by asking me to draft this contract?"

In contrast, here's what the feedback-giver might say when practicing Clean Feedback: "When you emailed yesterday and asked me to draft a contract with one of our top suppliers (the evidence), I was surprised. I've never done something like this before. I thought you might not be happy with my performance and might want me to prove myself (the inference). I didn't want to give up too soon, so I didn't say anything. But now, I feel insecure and don't know whether I can ask for help (the impact). I would like to clear this situation up."

Clean Feedback ensures that you stay truthful and that your message is as simple as possible. It reduces defensiveness and eases communication, which can deepen relationships. When an organization introduces Clean Feedback, it helps everyone to speak up earlier, then learn and improve faster.

Works great for: Personal issues and ones that could become emotionally complicated.

Trust the Process

Thomas J. Watson, the chairman and CEO of IBM from 1914 to 1956, once refused to fire an employee who made a mistake, even though it cost the company $600,000. Why? Because he said that the mistake was an investment in the employee's training; the last thing he wanted to do was let him go.

When assigning vertical slices of work to team members for the first time, you might worry that it's too much responsibility. The thing is, they *will* fail. If they've only ever worked in a traditional, task-specific structure, vertical slicing will be completely new, but that's okay. If you help them slice work vertically into small slices, their failure will have a much smaller impact. It won't cost $600,000. And they will learn faster.

As a leader, you're there to help them when they make mistakes, to give them feedback so they can learn. Eventually, they'll trust their own abilities, and you'll trust each other.

This trust has the power to reshape how the whole company operates.

Grow Your Nonprofit's Challenge

Let's look at how Thomas from Grow Your Nonprofit plans to campaign for new applications from small nonprofits. Such campaigns typically involve sending newsletters to various nonprofits and raising awareness through social media channels. It also usually involves engaging previous participants who are willing to promote the new program. What's unpredictable is determining which strategies will be most effective in attracting the appropriate applicants.

Thomas previously approached such projects by assigning separate tasks to each member of his six-person team. One person was responsible for drafting one newsletter, while another would create a different one. Someone else would source photos, and yet another team member would draft a letter to address partners and former participants. After the individual tasks were completed, Thomas would review the pieces and sometimes assemble the final newsletter himself before sending it out. Upon receiving replies, he would delegate the workload to individual colleagues for follow-up.

This year, Thomas wants to try a different approach, one that doesn't require so much micromanaging. He starts by slicing the work vertically together with his team and ensuring they understand what each slice means. Here are a few examples of their vertical slices:

- Newsletter targeting nonprofits only in rural areas
- Newsletter focusing on nonprofits for the elderly
- Personalized letter and follow-up to a top donor, Mrs. Schmidt

Under Thomas's new plan, team members will work together to produce the newsletters without his oversight. They'll share ideas about layout, stories, photos, and the placement of the application for the nonprofits. Then they'll edit each other's work, share feedback, and send the newsletter out themselves.

Because the team has to coordinate their work closely, they meet daily and share what they've completed and what they are still working on. They have far more detailed insight into each other's work than ever before, and by the end of the first week, they send out the two different newsletters and the personalized letter to Mrs. Schmidt.

But when Thomas and his team come together to assess the impact of their work, they realize they made a mistake. They didn't enable tracking, so they don't know how many people opened their newsletters nor how many clicked on the embedded links.

As a result, Thomas helps the team establish a feedback infrastructure for newsletters: he shows them how to enable tracking and provides them with the data from previous campaigns so they can compare the outcome of their newsletters with those from previous years.

Their top donor, Mrs. Schmidt, received her email, requested further details, and used her personal network to spread the message. Plus, the whole process was much faster than when Thomas was coordinating every piece of communication with her.

However, working together closely creates vulnerabilities. Imagine having everyone around you knowing how your work is going every single day and giving you their opinion about whether it's good or not.

This sort of radical accountability can bring up all sorts of anxieties and insecurities. *Are they criticizing me? Do they think I'm too slow? Or just no good?* To address these personal and process-related topics, Thomas and his team schedule a biweekly meeting.

The team took on new work, and through this process, they learned to become a self-managed team. They still made mistakes, and sometimes Thomas still had to be the one to send out a personal reply to some important partners, but they continued to improve. Because he didn't have to micromanage anymore, Thomas could focus on the big picture.

Two key aspects of Thomas's story are worth highlighting:

- Teams that work closely together and learn from their results on a regular basis benefit from separating their learning into two meetings: (1) to review the results and their impact (time for external learning; see Chapter 3), and (2) to reflect on how they work together (time for internal learning).
- As teams become more self-organized and work on vertical slices of a larger project, their leaders have more capacity to prioritize and determine which work is most valuable.

Prioritization, in fact, may be the greatest benefit of slicing vertically. The next chapter will dive deeper into why and how this works.

- ▶ Feedback is an emotionally demanding topic within organizations and requires attention.

- ▶ Slicing work vertically helps reduce risk for each individual slice, as well as increases feedback frequency.

- ▶ The most important leadership challenge is to create infrastructure that ensures feedback is given and received.

6

Prioritize and Work Smarter

So far, you've seen some of the ways you can increase productivity through vertical slicing. For instance, self-organization decreases management overhead and increases ownership, and shortened feedback loops speed up external and internal learning. Shortened feedback loops are most useful when unpredictability is high, because they alert you when a project is going offtrack.

But that's just part of the story. Maybe the biggest impact on productivity that vertical slicing offers is that with it you are able to prioritize what's most important.

Not Everything is of Equal Value

In 1896, Vilfredo Pareto observed that 80 percent of the land in Italy was owned by only 20 percent of the population. Today, his principle is evident in our lives in a variety of scenarios. The number of recipes you use out of a cookbook. The artists you listen to on Spotify or games you play on a console. How wealth or income is distributed among a population.

> The **Pareto principle** states that 80 percent of results come from 20 percent of effort.

It applies to your professional work too. Whether you're a small business or a multinational operation, more often than not you'll find that 20 percent of your clients are responsible for 80 percent of your revenue. Likewise, most complaints come from a small percentage of customers. A small percentage of projects delivers the most impact.

The most economically successful companies are the ones able to leverage the Pareto principle to their benefit. Amazon, for example, is famous for knowing when to say no so they can prioritize what's most profitable. The company kills products all the time.

In 2015, Amazon killed the Amazon Fire Phone due to poor sales, even though they spent several years developing it. Amazon Explore, a platform that connected customers with local tour guides and activities, was launched in 2016 and discontinued in 2018. Amazon Dash, a small Wi-Fi connected device that allowed customers to reorder household items by pressing a button, debuted in 2015 and was discontinued in 2018.

But most organizations don't operate this way. Instead, ideas are discussed for far too long. Then, once a project is started and it's clear that it isn't going to work, they plod on anyway.

Having Amazon's readiness to get rid of what's not working is great, but vertical slicing enables you to delete small parts instead of doing away with an entire project. That way, you can continuously shift toward what's most valuable.

Leverage the 80/20 Rule

Even though many managers are aware of the 80/20 rule, they can't apply it because they're hamstrung by traditional processes.

To illustrate this, let's look at the development of

something that you probably use and are likely frustrated by: the television remote. What on earth are all of those buttons for? I normally use only five: one for on and off, the up and down buttons for changing channels, and the ones for changing volume.

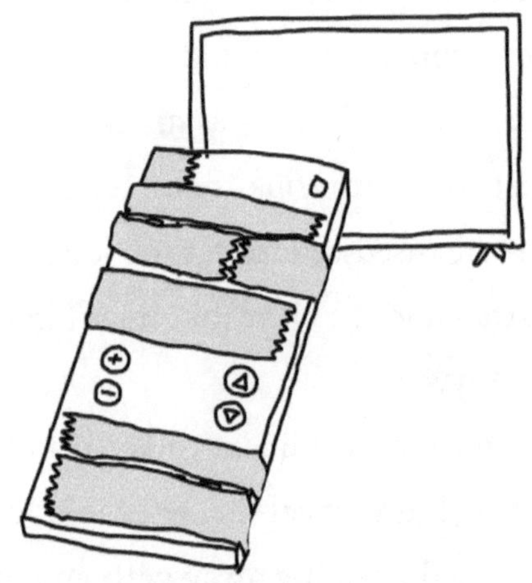

Fig. 12: An easy-to-understand remote control.

Think about how this multibutton remote came to be. Someone first analyzed the various functions that the remote may need to trigger. The remote control was designed to enable all these functions, and once those functions were implemented, it was put on the market. This is the classical, horizontal process of project management, which doesn't identify the all-important 20 percent—the five buttons that you need most of the time.

Imagine a different process. First, there's a remote prototype with just one button: to turn the TV on and off. Testers no longer have to get up and down to control the power, but they still have to change channels with a dial. The next iteration: a remote with three buttons, one to turn it on/off and the other to change channels. After receiving more tester feedback, two more buttons are added, for increasing or decreasing volume.

Like me, most testers would be satisfied with this simple, easy-to-navigate, five-button remote. If the remote manufacturer stopped there, instead of adding twenty-five or so other buttons, imagine all the time and money they could save on production. Imagine how much less frustration users would have, since they wouldn't have to figure out what a ton of other buttons are for.

Many companies look for ways to use the Pareto principle, but it requires that work be structured around small, vertical slices. When organizations that are slicing work horizontally try to apply the 80/20 rule, it doesn't work.

You cannot just do the most important 20 percent of an activity. A spoon that's only been washed 20 percent is still dirty, even though the largest pieces of food have been removed. If only 20 percent of a canvas is painted, it's still not complete, even though the main character is visible. When you do only a fraction of an activity (i.e., a horizontal slice), you get a low-quality result.

When you start vertically slicing projects, it changes your perspective on the work. It changes the conversation. Instead of being time- and budget-focused, you begin to prioritize value.

Stay Value-Focused Versus Output-Focused

If you're responsible for horizontally slicing the production of television remotes, your only focus will be on getting them designed, manufactured, boxed, and shipped on time and within budget. In contrast, if you're slicing the work vertically, you'll ask yourself: *Is this button necessary? Where is the best place to put the on/off button? Where should the one for channels go?*

Horizontally sliced work is output-focused; it's about speed and efficiency. Vertically sliced work is about value. *How can we deliver this product with greater impact? What increases customer satisfaction and retention and reduces complaints?*

At one of my workshops, a participant shared how

he shifted his thinking from output-focused to value-focused with a personal project he'd been struggling with. He'd bought a country house so his family could spend weekends away from the city, and when they weren't there, he wanted to rent it out as an Airbnb. But the house wasn't ready, not for his family or short-term rentals. It needed work. A lot of it.

Like most people, he approached the renovation process in a traditional way: he met with an architect and a contractor, then approved their bids for costs and deadlines. But not long after work started, problems arose. Faulty plumbing was uncovered behind a wall, and a plumber had to be called in to fix it before the project could continue. Then, there was a problem with the electrical wiring, and the project was held up once more while an electrician came out to make the repairs. The project was so unpredictable that costs and schedules were soon out of control.

After experiencing so many difficulties, he decided to go another route: hiring a contractor who did it all. The contractor had a cross-functional business where all of the specialists—in flooring, walls, plumbing, electrical, etc.—approached the entire project as a team. Instead of renovating the entire house at once, and by specialty, the team took a vertical approach. They worked room by room, starting on a new one only after they'd finished another.

In the short term, it cost more to do it this way, but the value was much higher. After a couple of weeks, one bedroom, a small bathroom, and the kitchen became habitable, so the owner's family was able to start enjoying the house. He even started renting out the finished portion. Month after month, one room after another became usable, increasing the family's comfort and the rent he could receive from visitors.

Perhaps even more significant, the process was no longer stressful. When unforeseen problems like cracked walls, faulty plumbing, or nonfunctioning wiring arose during renovation, the team of experts consulted with each other and then with him. Together, they quickly decided what to do and fixed the problems.

This is a terrific example of how self-organization reduces stress for managing unpredictable projects. It also shows how focusing on delivering value versus focusing on budget and deadlines often ends up being cheaper overall.

Fig. 13: Maximizing value by renovating an old country house one room at a time (below) versus all the rooms at once (above).

So, What Constitutes Value?

Value is defined by what various groups of stakeholders consider valuable. There are two different kinds of stakeholders:

- The people we are doing our work for, like customers, users, members, investors, or citizens. *How can we improve their experience?*
- The people within our organization who are doing the work and are affected by the project. *How does the project serve them? How does it serve our organization's long-term mission?*

Let's look at a couple of examples of what might constitute value in different projects:

Bread & More

- ✓ *Value to customers*: softer and more delicious croissants, higher satisfaction
- ✓ *Value to organization*: higher revenue with higher customer retention; on the production side, easily learned processes, which make the business run more smoothly and with fewer interruptions

Department of Emergency Support and Housing

- ✓ *Value to refugees*: basic housing; the ability to focus on integrating into society (e.g., learn a new language, find work, send kids to school); no conflict with other residents
- ✓ *Value to organization*: accelerate the process and lower the cost per inhabitant; improve ability to quickly increase or decrease the number of housing units
- ✓ *Value to citizens*: housing the homeless so they don't have to live on the streets

Grow Your Nonprofit

- ✓ *Value to applicants*: get professional help to grow their operations and optimize their processes; connect with other like-minded nonprofits
- ✓ *Value to organization*: increase the number of people successfully working in nonprofits worldwide; increase their supporter network and awareness for their brand; secure future funding

Bringing different stakeholder perspectives together to define value is commonly referred to as "stakeholder management." With a traditional, horizontally sliced project, stakeholder management plays a more important role in the planning phase of a project and becomes less important after implementation. With vertically sliced work, it's another story.

Every project I've ever worked on has had a different answer to the question, "What is valuable?" And the answer always changes over time. That's why, for uncertain projects, you need to continuously work with stakeholders to decide what's valuable.

Each vertical slice of a project contributes value in a different way. One slice may serve the needs of several stakeholders to a small extent, while another serves only one group but makes a big difference to them. Another slice may not be urgent but promises a large increase in revenue when it's done, while another has a hard deadline of one week in order to meet a contractual obligation. When prioritizing, you need to consider all these different variables at once.

So how do you decide what has the highest priority?

Typically, the more benefits something brings, the greater the amount of harm that it prevents, or the more urgent it is, the higher its priority should be. However, when prioritizing work, there's still one variable people often get wrong: risk.

Do High-Risk Slices First

With unpredictable projects, some parts are always riskier than others. In this case, riskier means that they are less familiar to you and your team.

Most people start with the less-risky parts of a project because they're safer. Because they're what they know and they don't want the value of their work to be endangered. Then they work their way up to the riskier ones.

It's a common pitfall.

It seems counterintuitive, but the higher the risk, the more important it is to do it first. In an unpredictable project, you don't actually know how the different parts may depend on one another. So if you leave the riskiest parts until the end and a failure occurs, everything you've already done might be in jeopardy. In contrast, if you assess the highest-risk items and do them first, one vertical slice of work at a time, you not only accomplish something you are unfamiliar with, but you also reduce risk for the whole project.

When working with unpredictability, apply vertical slicing continuously, leveraging the Pareto principle, to be more productive and achieve higher-quality results. Ensuring the quality of your work is a critical part of the process, so we'll discuss how to do so in the next chapter.

▶ With vertical slicing, you can leverage the 80/20 rule to increase productivity.

▶ Focusing on value instead of timelines or budgets helps you deliver unpredictable projects faster and at lower costs in the long run.

▶ Determining the most valuable vertical slice in any given project is a continuous leadership responsibility in unpredictable environments.

▶ The riskiest parts of the project need to be addressed first.

7

Keep Quality High

People dread the quality assurance process, especially in organizations dealing with high unpredictability. But why does the mention of the word "quality" evoke such unease? Because when you deal with unpredictability, traditional strategies to ensure quality fail.

In a horizontally sliced project, the overall quality is a result of precise planning up front and thorough testing at the end. When unpredictable projects suddenly change direction, and uncover important, missed elements along the way, this strategy is doomed to fail.

It's not always obvious, but the way we manage quality is deeply connected with the idea of vertical slicing. Whenever we are doing something well, we are fulfilling two major criteria at the same time:

- Doing the right *thing*
- Doing the thing *right*

These two criteria are independent, and only one of them is related to quality. How do you know which one? Think of what happens when one of them is met while the other is not.

You can do the wrong thing but do it well, such as serving a high-quality dish that no one ordered. In contrast, you can do the right thing but do it poorly, such as serving undercooked potatoes.

In the dinner party example, doing the right *thing* means preparing the correct dishes—the burger, the hummus, the tiramisu. The description of the vertical slices even specifies exactly what kind of burger is needed—cheeseburger with two patties and extra bacon. Nothing new here.

However, doing the thing *right* at the dinner party means following a checklist of *all of the activities* that need to be performed as you prepare each dish. For instance, you want to use only clean knives and wash them after cutting meats to reduce the risk of food contamination. You want to make sure your ingredients are fresh and not beyond their "best by" date. This checklist is called the "Definition of Done."

The Definition of Done is agreed upon when the work starts, but it also evolves over time as you uncover more about your project and receive feedback on what you've done. It helps people doing the work to collaborate and ensure their work is meeting quality standards. It also provides security to stakeholders, since they can always rely on this checklist to have been ticked off.

When organizations start to comply with the Definition of Done for each vertical slice, it changes not just how they slice work, but also how they perform it.

How You Work Will Change

When organizations horizontally slice work, they're accustomed to having a large amount of time to check for quality in the late stages of a project. But because vertical slices are typically delivered within weeks, team members are required to check all of a project's moving parts quickly and more frequently.

This increase in effort is often the most difficult part of transitioning to vertical slicing, but fear not: organizations that have taken on this challenge have adjusted by finding new ways of working.

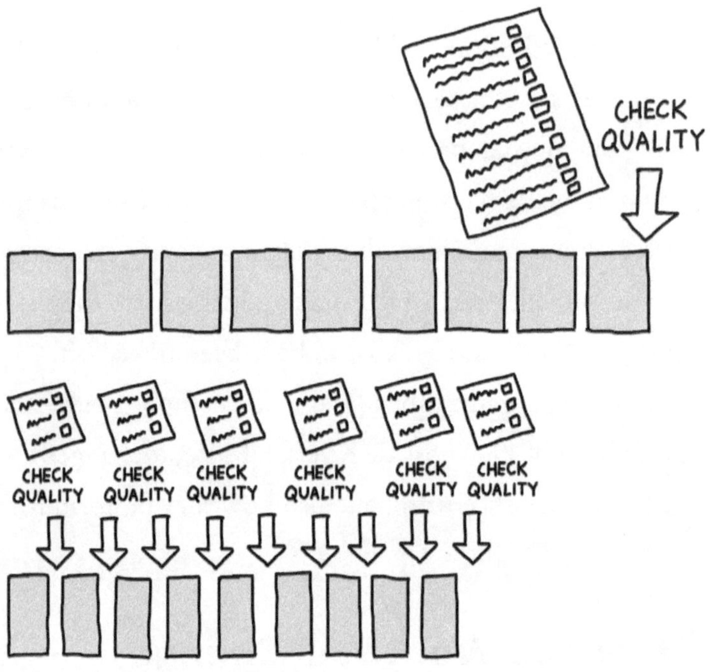

Fig. 14: Quality checks need to be done more frequently with vertically sliced work. Teams develop their own tools to reduce the associated effort.

When Susan, Jenny, and Thomas switched to vertically sliced work, they also created new techniques to keep quality high. Each one of their stories illustrates how the Definition of Done ensures quality, as well as how teams create new practices to check quality much more often. Some of their strategies may work for your projects.

Ensuring Quality at Bread & More

As we discussed, Susan's team spent two weeks testing croissants baked in different ovens at ten store branches, which was one vertical slice of work. Then, they spent another two weeks examining the influence of display cases on the croissant's freshness, a second vertical slice. When they discovered that the display cases were the issue, the third vertical slice was to replace them and verify that it improved the croissants.

No matter what the team learned, there were some nonnegotiables to check off the Definition of Done list:

- Did the new production process meet all government food and safety guidelines and/or regulations?
- Did the production costs for one croissant stay within budget?
- Did the resulting croissants feel, smell, and taste the way croissants should taste according to the team members? Immediately after baking, one hour later, five hours later?

All of these questions needed to be answered *each time* any one of the vertical slices above were in play.

Ensuring compliance with government food and safety regulations within two weeks in ten bakeries wasn't easy in the beginning. But one team member was an expert in this area, and they zeroed in on the parts of the regulations that were relevant to their project. From there, they created a short and simplified list that everyone on the team could go through within one hour.

The team also created a spreadsheet with all of the factors that might influence the production cost of making croissants, which they needed to keep below a certain threshold. This too became a tool they used with each iteration.

In short, the team created their Definition of Done, a master list that incorporated all of the quality-related activities that needed to be performed before their vertical slice could be considered complete. Once they created the abbreviated food and safety regulations checklist and the cost spreadsheet, ensuring high quality every two weeks became much easier.

Ensuring Quality at the Department of Emergency Support and Housing

With the challenge to find housing for ten people in the first week and for twenty in the second (vertical slices), Jenny and her team had to act fast. And because they work for a government organization, it was critical that all aspects of the project met quality standards.

Some of the highest priorities included these:

- Following occupancy regulations and laws specific to housing, such as the number of square feet required per person
- Assessing the housing cost per person
- Accurately documenting all formal decisions, in case any of them were challenged in court

Because such a project had never been approached this way before, the team had to come up with their own process and create their own checklists. But that was only part of what they needed to do. They also had to check the building to see whether it could potentially add new residents, and if so, how. They needed to get consent from current residents, as well as agreement from the potential new residents. Then they needed to obtain short-term furnishings for the apartments.

Jenny's team self-organized and came up with a solution. They created a template to keep track of all of the requirements and decisions related to the project's first vertical slice, increasing the density of one building. They took it one step further by simplifying and listing only the specific parts of the laws and requirements that pertained to their projects, so they could be easily and quickly checked. They also rephrased and simplified all the legalese so they could quickly glance at a template and determine if they were in compliance. By creating these tools, Jenny and her team were able to save time from one building to the next.

Ensuring Quality at Grow Your Nonprofit

To attract applicants, Thomas's team worked on several newsletters to different target groups and personalized letters to top partners. Each of these vertical slices had different requirements, but they all shared a set of common quality criteria:

- Logos of all donors must be well placed and visible.
- Corporate identity of the organizations needs to be complied with.
- Stories must be written in simple, understandable language, and they need to be supported by fitting images.
- Font must be large enough that it's accessible to anyone with a visual impairment.

Traditionally, one person would write the first draft of the newsletter, and then the draft would be peer-reviewed by someone else. Once they reached an agreement about what the newsletter should look and sound like, the text would be fleshed out, and the images would be searched and inserted. A shareable file with comments and notes would always be passed around.

In this scenario, different versions of a file would exist simultaneously. Once each was edited and reviewed, they would need to be merged, which would sometimes lead to misunderstandings. In addition, one person would usually have to wait for another to finish their work, which made it difficult to meet the quality criteria for the production and distribution of several newsletters—especially within one week.

Instead of continuing to work within this outmoded, time-consuming process, Thomas's team switched to an online word-processing system where the document could be posted and open to edits and comments from all members of the team at the same time. That way, changes were made and accepted right away. Everyone could literally be on the same page, no file-merging needed. With simultaneous collaboration, the work could be done much faster, and the elements that defined the newsletter's quality, its Definition of Done, could be checked by everyone on the team.

Definition of Done Improves with Time

In these three scenarios, different strategies helped speed up the quality assurance process:

- Writing short, simple checklists, tailored to the specific work
- Creating tools that automated parts of the process
- Enabling simultaneous teamwork by using new technology or changing processes

As we've discussed, typically an initial Definition of Done is agreed upon before a project begins, but it's never perfect from the start. It evolves over time. There are two factors that contribute to this evolution: (1) the team finds better ways to meet existing quality criteria, or (2) quality defects are uncovered, and the team adds new criteria to address these deficiencies in the future.

Throughout this book, we've focused largely on making the principles behind slicing tangible and easy to understand, both by using examples from a variety of circumstances and by discussing useful tools where necessary. Now, in the final chapter, you will learn the main steps of slicing projects so that you can begin to apply the art of slicing to your own work.

▶ When slicing vertically, teams use the Definition of Done to ensure the quality of each slice individually.

▶ Checking quality needs to be done much more frequently than in traditional work, so teams will develop their own tools and practices to do the work.

▶ The Definition of Done is agreed upon at the start and evolves throughout the project.

How to Vertically Slice Your Project

Slicing works for any project, large or small. If you follow the process outlined in this chapter, you will end up with a useful plan for whatever vertical slices you hope to create. And perhaps most importantly, you will have a clear idea of what you hope to achieve with each slice—why it's useful—so that you can verify whether you are making progress.

Before we dive into the weeds, let's begin with the end in mind. What does it look like to navigate an unpredictable project?

Several centuries ago, navigators in the Age of Exploration were in a similar situation. They had a goal, a map, and tools to help them find their position—and quite an unpredictable journey ahead of them. Once they set out, they had to make daily decisions to stay on course.

Sometimes, the voyage would be relatively calm; the navigator would mark a course and set sail for days in the right direction. Other times, the navigator would adapt to the situation in front of them, such as a subtle underwater current or a looming wave, using incomplete information.

Fig. 15: Navigating an unpredictable project is like navigating a nineteenth-century ship. You have a goal and a map, and with those, you must decide how to approach what's right in front of you.

Slicing is much like navigating a ship. To succeed, you need a few key ingredients:

1. **A goal.** Where do you want to be in the end?
2. **A map.** This is your understanding of the terrain of your journey, where you can draw a path to the friendly shores of your destination. Your map consists of (1) the different outcomes that contribute to your goal; (2) clearly defined slices so you know what results you need to create; and (3) knowledge of the risks so you have a better understanding of where to expect unpredictability.
3. **A process.** This will help you understand where you are on the map, how you will use your map to define the next step toward your goal, and how you will take the next step.

Before we get started, one last note: As you're working through each step, let "good enough" be your operating principle. For example, as soon as you feel your goal statement is good enough, take it and move on to the next step. It's much better to spend one hour making a plan and one hour revising it than two hours making it initially.

Of course, as with any new practice, there is a learning curve, but you'll get better every time you slice a project vertically. So let's move through the following steps, revisiting examples from throughout the book to illustrate these processes in action.

Step 1: State the Goal

Naturally, the first thing you need to be clear on in order to have any success is your goal. Here in Step 1, we will walk through some tips to ensure your goal is helpful. Even if you have been given a goal and aren't at liberty to set one yourself, you can use these tools to reframe your goal in a way that is more useful to you.

To begin crafting your goal statement, ask yourself two questions:

1. What do I hope to get out of this endeavor?
2. What would it look like on the other side if I were to get what I am hoping for?

Use your answers to define, shape, or reshape your goals so that you can create a goal statement that is more useful to you as you navigate unpredictability.

To see what a good goal statement looks like, let's return to some of our examples from previous chapters:

- Your friends are full and impressed by your cooking abilities by the end of the dinner party.
- Bread & More's 2024 croissant sales are 50 percent higher than they were in 2023.
- The Department of Emergency Support and Housing has found an additional five hundred places for refugees within existing buildings.
- Grow Your Nonprofit has helped open twenty new, successful nonprofits.

These are all examples of "good enough" goal statements. Why? They all have the ability to elicit a positive emotional response in the people involved in the project. A good goal statement puts a smile on your face. It makes you think, *Yes! This is what I want.*

Yes, it really can be that simple. Remember, you know more about your project than anyone else. When your goal statement elicits a positive emotional response, that's your gut telling you that you are on the right track.

Too often, a manager and their team will look at a goal and feel confused. The goal feels abstract or otherwise hard to understand, and so they don't feel connected to it. If you find that you and your team aren't connecting with your goal, compare your goal to these common challenges:

- **Not concrete.** When the description of your goal is not concrete, it can be hard to get anyone to agree upon what you actually want to do. For instance, the goal "improve our team's communication" is vague. Some level of ambiguity is okay, but your goals should still clearly state a before/after where appropriate.
- **Action/output.** A goal shouldn't be the same as the output. That is, it shouldn't be the result of a vertical slice, like "I want a crispy duck on my dinner table." If you discover that your goal is focused on action/output, work to focus more on why the goal is useful. For instance, the goal statement, "I want my guests to be full and happy by the end of the evening" indicates why you set out to host a dinner party in the first place.
- **One-time behavior.** If the goal doesn't result in consistent change, then it's likely not the real, final goal. You can manipulate anyone into doing something once without it having any effect, like "Get the CEO to commission a sustainability

assessment." Instead, think about something systematic that you want to change. For instance, the goal statement, "The board of directors reviews the company's sustainability progress every quarter" indicates long-term change.

- **Introducing a tool.** Tool adoption, like "implementing a CRM," is very often an important part of a project. However, introducing a tool is never the goal in and of itself; the tool is only introduced in service of a greater goal. So an appropriate goal might be to "improve the company's ability to manage customer relationships."

After reviewing your goal statement, you may realize it suffers from one or more of these common challenges. If that's the case, then use the following questions to improve your goal statement:

1. What are you hoping to achieve with this action/output/behavior/tool?
2. How will you know it's achieved?

Once you've answered these questions, revise your goal statement until you've made it more tangible. As soon as your goal statement gives you that *yes!* feeling, move on to the next step. Remember: good enough is good enough.

However, if you later wake up in the middle of the night and realize you can further improve your goal statement, that's fine. Slicing is iterative, so you can always revisit and revise.

Step 2: Mapping Stakeholder Behaviors

Just like a navigator needs a map to understand what territory they want to cover, managers of a project need a map as well. Here in Step 2, you'll learn how to create it.

As you can see in Figure 16, your map will consist of three components: your goal, your outcomes, and the slices of work you will deliver to create the outcome. Right now, you'll focus on identifying outcomes and slices, starting with your goal statement.

Before we start, first I would like to give credit where it is due. The technique of mapping outcomes and slices to a given goal is commonly referred to as Impact Mapping, which was highly popularized by Gojko Adzic in his book of the same name.[6] I will summarize the practice here as it pertains to slicing.

Outcomes

For our purposes, outcomes can be defined as target behaviors by specific actors that contribute to your goal. To identify your target outcomes, focus on the *who* and *what*:

- Whose behavior matters?
- What behavior matters—and how could that behavior change in order to support your goal?

Often, there is more than one *who* and *what*. For instance, to meet their goal of increasing croissant sales, Bread & More could break down the *who* and *what* like so:

- Staff needs to bake higher-quality croissants.
- Logistic partners need to deliver more frozen, formed croissants on time.
- Existing clients need to become aware of improved croissants.

---

6   Gojko Adzic, *Impact Mapping: Making a Big Impact with Software Products and Projects* (Provoking Thoughts, 2012).

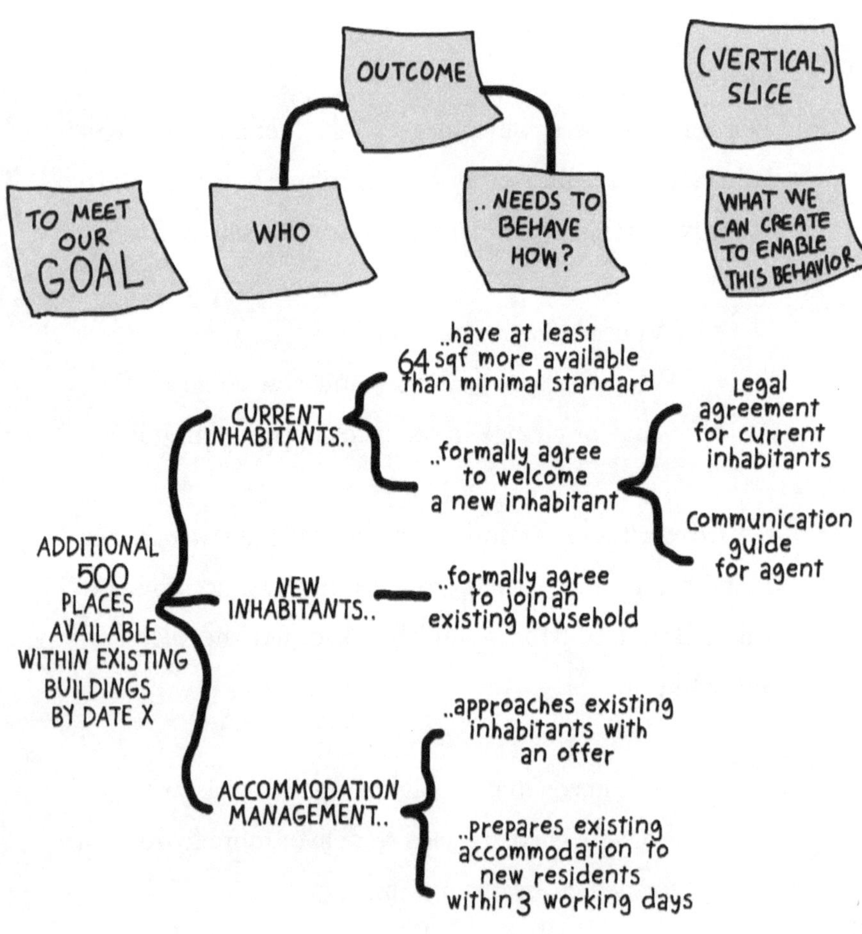

Fig. 16: An excerpt of the impact map for Jenny's project at the Department of Emergency Support and Housing.

For a more detailed example, let's go back to the story of Jenny at the Department of Emergency Support and Housing.

Jenny's goal was to find an additional five hundred places for refugees within existing buildings. This is a somewhat unconventional goal. Under normal circumstances, the Department of Emergency Support and Housing would acquire new buildings to house incoming refugees while maintaining minimal space requirements and standards of living. However, because there was an enormous influx of refugees, Jenny and her team couldn't find or build accommodations that met these space requirements in a timely manner. The typical response in this stressful situation would be to house the refugees in emergency shelters, but these shelters pose other challenges—chiefly, that refugees living in such accommodations find it much more difficult to integrate into society.

Mindful of the challenges posed by these shelters, Jenny and her team made it their goal to house the refugees in existing buildings. Doing so allowed them to circumvent the typical space requirements necessary for inhabitants, and the refugees benefited not only from the additional social support, but also from their proximity to town, where they were better positioned to find jobs.

To make her idea a reality, first Jenny created a map of outcomes and, ultimately, slices (see Figure 16). After identifying her team's goal, Jenny's next step was to identify the different actors who might influence that goal and the target behaviors for each:

1. **Current inhabitants**: Must have at least sixty-four square feet of space available above the minimal standard and must agree to welcome new inhabitants—or formally agree to welcome inhabitants even if they are low on space
2. **New inhabitants**: Must formally agree to join existing households
3. **Accommodation management**: Must approach existing inhabitants with an offer and then prepare existing accommodation for new residents within three days

Every combination of *who* and *how*—that is, who your actors are and how you need them to behave to achieve your goal—constitutes a target outcome. In this case, if current inhabitants agreed to welcome new refugees into their homes, that outcome would contribute to the larger goal of finding an additional five hundred places for refugees within existing buildings.

Slices

Once you have figured out the outcomes supporting your goal, next you will determine what slice you need to set in place in order to support this outcome.

Before we delve into this further, let's reiterate the difference between outcomes and slices or outputs. Outcomes are the behavior changes needed for your goal to be achieved. Slices are things we create to enable or enhance these behaviors. For example:

- In order to impress your guests at the dinner party, you wanted to cook a dish that tasted extraordinary.
- In order for Bread & More's bakers to deliver higher-quality croissants, Susan and her team wanted to put closed display cases in each store.
- In order for Jenny and her team to find housing for five hundred additional refugees, they needed to encourage current residents to invite those refugees into their homes.

Let's dive deeper into Jenny's example. To encourage current residents to welcome refugees into their homes, Jenny's team needed to focus on a variety of slices. For our purposes, we will focus on two:

1. A template for a legal agreement that all current
   residents would sign
2. A communication guide for all representatives
   of the management company to share

Each of these results represents a vertical slice—in other words, the final results of Jenny's work with her team (see Figure 16).

Remember that we have focused on only one outcome and one set of slices. But in order to build out a complete map for your own project, you will need to repeat this process for every outcome. Most likely, if you're doing this work correctly, this will result in a fairly large and complicated map.

In German, there is a word called *entblättern*, which means to take something densely packed—like a flower or a head of lettuce—and unpack it into its individual leaves or petals. That's essentially what you're doing when you create your map: you are unpacking the complicated, interrelated parts of your project so you can better understand how everything comes together. If your project is large, it's only natural for your map to be large as well.

Because you've created these maps in this particular way, you already know why each vertical slice is useful. Each was created as an idea of how to enhance a certain outcome that is connected to your goal. Further, everything you've created on your map is both pragmatic and testable; because you already know the outcome each vertical slice should produce, you can get feedback quickly on whether it's leading to your desired result.

Of course, with such a big map, the next question becomes this: What should you start with? In Step 3, we'll discuss how to prioritize your efforts.

How Will You Build Your Map?

As you can see from our conversation in Step 2, identifying target behaviors and outcomes can make your map get rather complicated rather quickly—and we identified only a small subset of them in Jenny's example!

To manage such a large amount of information, it's useful to have a visual tool. If you'd like, you can create your map on a whiteboard; just know that you're going to need a very large whiteboard. Personally, I've found virtual whiteboarding tools like miro.com, mural.com, or conceptboard.com to be much more effective and easier to manage.

Step 3: Prioritize the Unfamiliar

Now that you know your goal and have a map of the terrain, you need to lay an initial path for your journey. This path will most likely change because of what you learn when you take your initial steps, but how do you identify those initial steps in the first place?

As we discussed in Chapter 6, prioritization allows you to multiply the productivity of your teams several times over. This means staying value-focused and doing high-risk slices first. In the beginning of a project, these high-risk slices play a bigger role, so we're going to focus on them first.

High-Risk Slices

Before we dive in, let's take a moment to reiterate why focusing on high-risk slices is so important, since this approach is often counterintuitive to people at first.

The more unfamiliar you are with any new territory, the more likely you'll be surprised by what you find—and these surprises may render other previously achieved results useless. For example, imagine Jenny's team created a comprehensive communication guide and legal documentation as part of her process. These could be very valuable results, unless she and her team found they needed to significantly adapt their offer after speaking with current inhabitants. The sooner you identify and address potential surprises, the less likely you are to produce waste later on, and the quicker you'll be able to adapt.

To identify unknown and unfamiliar territories, scan your map. Look for outcomes and slices in your map that you or your organization have either never done before or have only done a few times (see Figure 17).

A note of caution: one of the most common mistakes I see organizations make at this step is to stay too general. Many claim to be experienced with an outcome or a slice while overlooking the details that make this particular situation unique. To counteract this tendency, be intentional when looking for unfamiliar parts.

To see this step in action, let's return once again to Jenny's efforts to find housing for incoming refugees. For the purposes of our discussion, I have limited this example to just the first two outcomes in our map: getting formal agreements from current inhabitants and new inhabitants.

Jenny's organization has extensive experience with getting formal agreements from the people they serve, but they had never made a request like this before—especially not under these circumstances, with this particular group of refugees, and with this particular management company.

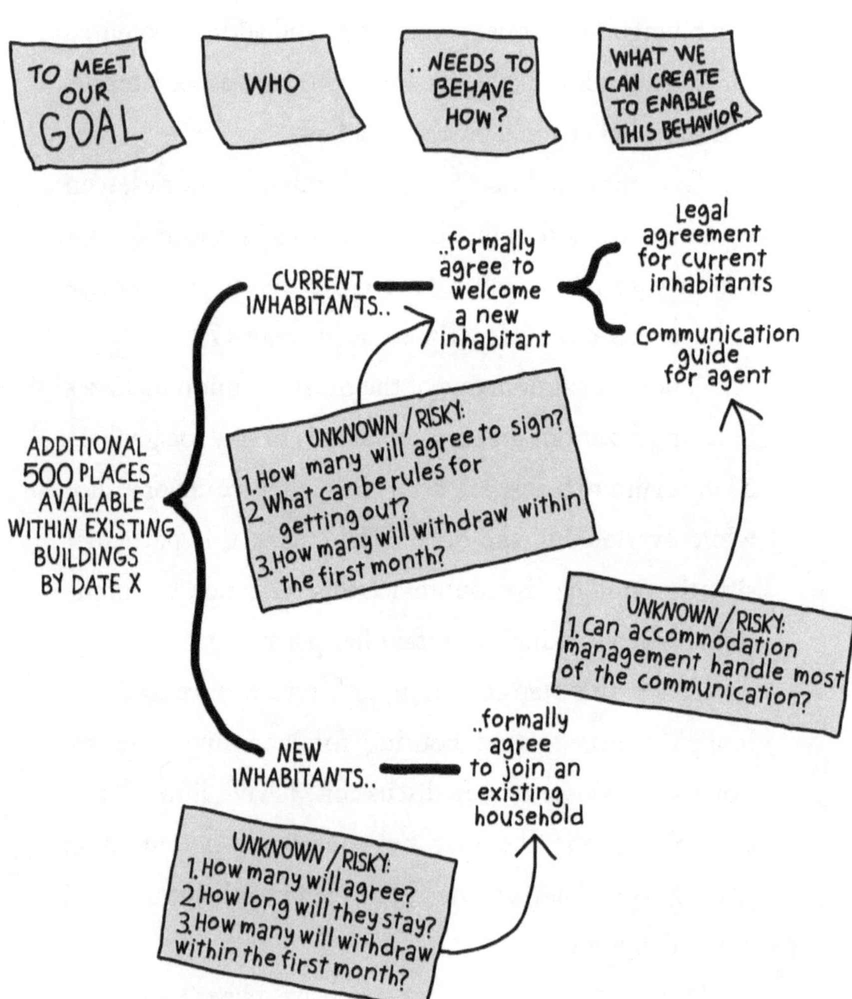

Fig. 17: Look for outcomes and slices in your impact map that you are least familiar with. List your open questions. Here is an example for Jenny's project.

They wondered, *Will the current inhabitants formally agree to these requests, or will they resist?*

Of course, this was just one of the unknowns they faced. Other unknowns included these:

- How many will agree to sign?
- What are the rules for getting out of the agreement?
- How many will withdraw within the first month?

These unknowns extended all the way to the vertical slice as well. For instance, one of the slices identified in Step 2 was to create a communication guide for the agents. But would the staff at the current management company be able to handle this communication?

Each of these questions represents a mission-critical point in the process. The sooner you can deliver a slice that tests these critical points, the sooner you will know whether and how you can deliver on your project. If the feedback is positive and you're able to achieve the outcome, then the risk is gone. However, if the feedback is negative, you can learn, change your map, and determine your next steps. In either scenario, the team should learn something valuable and move forward with the project.

High-Value Slices

Once all mission-critical points have been tested and no longer pose a significant risk, your next priority is to deliver all the highest-value slices. Of course, in order to stay value-focused, you need to be clear about what constitutes value in your project. (You can find examples of what "value" might mean to your project in Chapter 6.)

Working this way, you'll come to a point where most of the valuable slices have been delivered and the results speak for themselves. At that point, you can consider stopping the project and congratulating yourself on a job well done.

As beautiful as this process sounds, it falls apart when you aren't able to deliver and get feedback on small slices every couple of weeks. This is the final and core part of the art of slicing work.

Step 4: Slice Small

For most projects, as you begin to execute, you will likely discover that the slices you've identified in Steps 2 and 3 are too large. They will take months—or even up to a year—to deliver!

To keep delivering results within two to three weeks,

you need to slice smaller. As you will see in the following examples, there are several different strategies to do that.

1. Focus on a Segment of a Group First

The first strategy to slice smaller is reducing your goal. This doesn't mean changing the direction of your project but achieving the goal for a smaller segment of customers/affected people. Usually, you will find that this requires significantly less work.

Let's return to Jenny and her team from the Department of Emergency Support and Housing. They had a stated goal of finding an additional five hundred places for refugees within existing buildings, but that was too great of a goal to attempt all at once. So in the beginning, they narrowed their focus down to a much more specific group of refugees. The question then was this: How should they segment the group?

This is the question any project team must ask when slicing a goal. While the answer will depend on the specific circumstances of the project, here are some guiding questions:

1. **What different situations do the people in your target group face before being affected by your project?** Typically, you'll find segments

with different problems, which require different approaches. By focusing on one such segment at a time, you reduce your work.

2. **Are there segments from or in locations that are also significantly different?** The same question can be asked for people who require our attention at different times.

In Figure 18, you can see how Jenny and her team used these questions to reduce her goal. Instead of focusing on housing five hundred refugees all at once, they decided to start by housing only ten mothers with one child apiece. These mothers were from Ukraine and had arrived within the past month.

Instead of trying to house refugees of all ages, genders, and abilities, they focused solely on solving the need for one specific group. This allowed them to narrow their criteria for which existing inhabitants to talk to, to create a much more specific communication strategy, and to more intentionally prepare homes for newcomers.

This isn't to say that Jenny rejected the larger goal. Rather, she and her team focused on delivering part of the goal and learning from the process before working on delivering the rest of the goal. Once they successfully housed the first segment, they were able to turn their attention to the remaining refugee segments.

1. Concentrating on Smaller Customer Segments

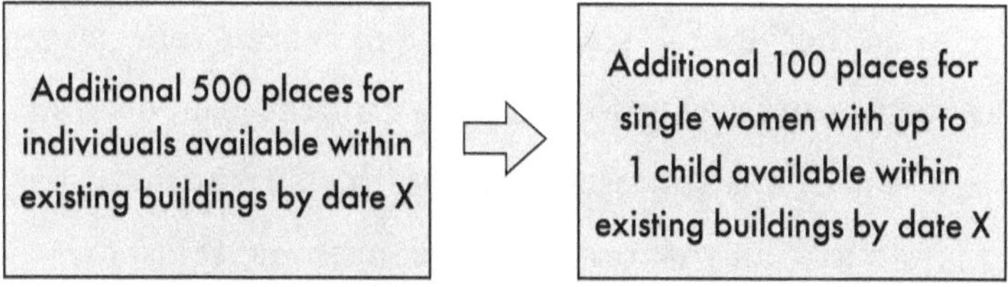

a. even more specific situation/problem

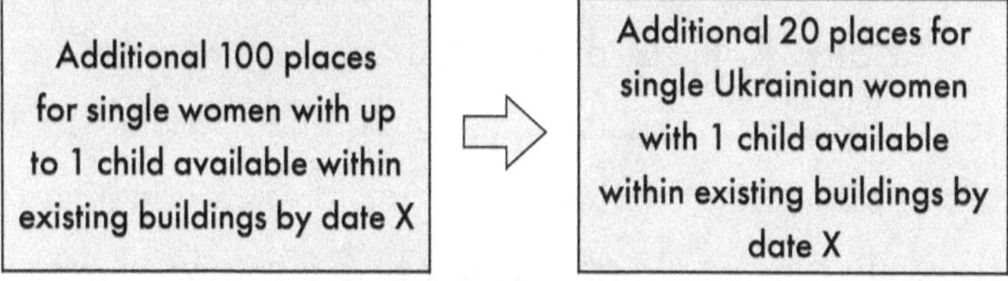

b. geographically or temporarily limited customer segment

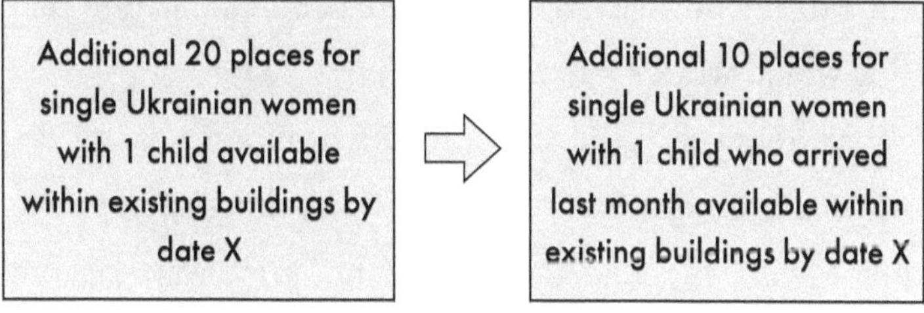

Fig. 18: Strategies to reduce the vertical slice
by concentrating on a smaller segment.

2. Start with a Partial Outcome

Sometimes, reducing the goal doesn't reduce the amount of work enough for your team to deliver a result within a couple of weeks. In that case, you need to slice further.

Another useful strategy is looking at your target outcomes and seeing whether you can reduce an outcome in a way that is still useful. Again, this doesn't mean you want to toss out your original target outcome. It just means that if you can create a partial outcome first, you might learn something that will help you complete the rest.

In Step 2, Jenny determined that in order for her team to meet their housing goal, they would need current inhabitants to formally agree to a new inhabitant. Typically, this would take longer than a couple of weeks to get done. Since this was one of the riskiest places in the project, however, she wanted to see an indication that this would work sooner.

So Jenny reduced the outcome from a formal agreement to an indication of interest by booking an appointment with the management team. That way, current inhabitants wouldn't have to sign a contract or anything binding; they would just have to show a willingness to consider the idea.

Jenny and her team also combined strategies here. For instance, in addition to reducing the outcome, they reduced the group by asking only current female inhabitants if they were interested in welcoming single mothers with one child.

2. Start with a Partial Outcome

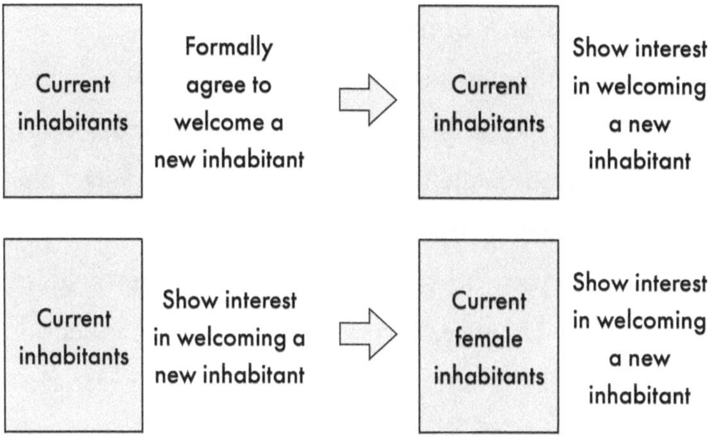

Current inhabitants — Formally agree to welcome a new inhabitant ⟹ Current inhabitants — Show interest in welcoming a new inhabitant

Current inhabitants — Show interest in welcoming a new inhabitant ⟹ Current female inhabitants — Show interest in welcoming a new inhabitant

Fig. 19: Strategies to reduce the vertical slice by concentrating on a partial outcome.

The agreement represented just a small piece of the outcome, but it was much easier to achieve—and it provided valuable information about whether the remaining inhabitants would be willing to formally agree later. After all, if no one in the smaller group showed interest in making an appointment, then certainly no one would sign anything binding. The team would need to change their offering before attempting again.

This process may result in dead ends at times, but it ultimately saves you from wasted effort. By starting with a partial outcome, you can test your idea earlier with less of an impact.

3. Try Simpler Means

So far, we've discussed how to slice smaller by reducing the goal or reducing the outcome. But in most cases, these strategies alone are still not enough to deliver the first slice in a couple of weeks.

Another way to slice smaller is to target simpler means. For instance, instead of producing an entire communication guide for all the agents of the management company, Jenny's team decided to create a one-page flyer that offered guidance on what to say and what not to say. It was produced in a couple of days and led to results within a couple of weeks.

3. Try Simpler or Fewer Means to Achieve the Outcome

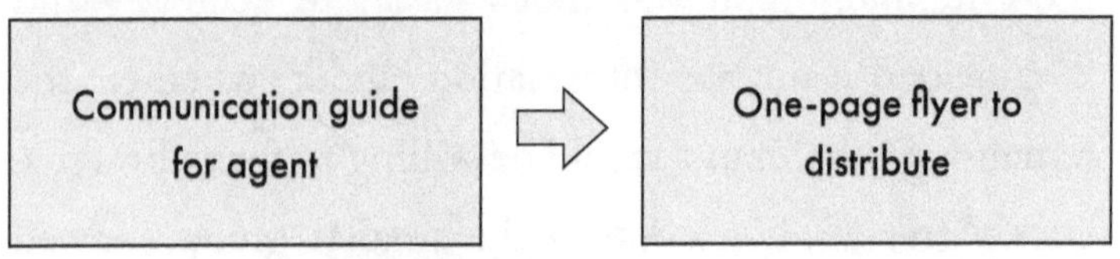

Fig. 20: Strategies to reduce the vertical slice by trying simpler or fewer means to achieve the same outcome.

This strategy is known as *dimensional planning.*[7]

Typically, when we work to solve a problem, we focus on creating the best possible solution to that problem. For instance, if we want to connect two cities with roads, the first solution that pops up in our heads is constructing a highway. But do you need a highway right away? What would a solution with simpler means look like? A city road? A small-town road? Even a dirt road? Again, you may still want the highway eventually, but if the dirt road delivers results more quickly so that you can learn and iterate, then it's worth considering.

What slice your team is building is very specific to your project, but whatever it is, ask yourself this: Is the current idea we have a highway or a city road? If so, what would be the equivalent of a small-town road or a dirt road?

With that said, we never slice just for the sake of slicing. We slice when we realize that we can't deliver our next slice within a couple of weeks. If the slice is already small enough—for instance, if you can reasonably produce and test a communication guide in two weeks—then there's no need to slice further.

---

7   *Dimensional planning* was first introduced at XP-Days Benelux in 2007 by Koen Van Exem and Walter Hesius.

4. Use Prototypes to Prove the Outcome Is Achievable

Sometimes even simplifying your means doesn't reduce the work enough. In that case, you can use prototypes—things you know you'll eventually throw away—to reduce a risk or to test something significant in an unfamiliar territory.

For instance, Jenny decided that creating a one-pager made more sense than producing an entire communication guide. Taking the idea of simplifying the slice even further, she decided to create a prototype of that flyer.

Instead of spending the time and effort to design an eye-catching document, her team created the first version in a word processor. It wasn't pretty, but the prototype document was good enough to test—in this case, testing means distributing it to residents of a single building. If the test was effective, Jenny and her team knew they could create a standardized flyer with more professional design elements.

The "Fake Door" Prototype

Another approach involves creating what's known as a *"fake door" prototype*, a concept originating from the lean startup movement but now widely used in various settings. This involves producing something that resembles your intended future offering—the "fake door"—to see if people will attempt to use it. If they do, it indicates that the actual product is worth developing.

Fake door prototypes are valuable for addressing uncertainty in your outcome, and they're startlingly simple to execute. Even Jenny and her team made use of a fake door prototype. They distributed a flyer to all current inhabitants, asking whether they were interested in welcoming another refugee into their home and, if so, requesting that they send a message to a designated email address.

This prototype requires very little work—far less than creating a legal agreement, a communication guide, or anything else like that. All Jenny and her team had to do was gauge interest by collecting replies. Once they collected enough replies to prove their inhabitants were interested in welcoming new refugees, then they could go about the work of actually producing the agreement and other essentials needed to deliver their target outcomes.

The "Do Things That Don't Scale" Prototype

The last way to produce a prototype is through the "Do Things That Don't Scale" prototype, first introduced in 2013 by Paul Graham, a revolutionary thinker and mentor for entrepreneurs.[8] The crux of this approach is that once teams identify a slice to be too large to produce, they look for ways to get first results faster by deliberately doing more manual work themselves (a.k.a. things that don't scale).

For example, at the beginning of the project, Jenny and her team intended to create a communication guide for agents to use when talking with current inhabitants about their interest in offering some of their space to incoming refugees. This guide would absolutely be useful down the road, offering a scalable approach to effective communication. At the moment, however, they still didn't know whether this communication guide would work.

So before spending a ton of time producing a complex document that they might not need, Jenny and her team decided to take the "Do Things That Don't Scale" approach. They picked a building, headed out on their own, and spent the next several hours speaking one-on-one to about fifteen inhabitants about their

---

8   Paul Graham, "Do Things That Don't Scale," *Paul Graham* (blog), July 2013, http://paulgraham.com/ds.html. This approach is best described by Paul Graham. There are similar approaches referred to as "Concierging" or "Wizard of Oz," but I prefer this naming, as it is more descriptive and general.

plans. This approach wasn't scalable, but these initial conversations gave them some important information about their goal's feasibility, what language to use, and talking points that they could later include in their communication guide.

4. Use a Prototype to Prove the Outcome is Achievable

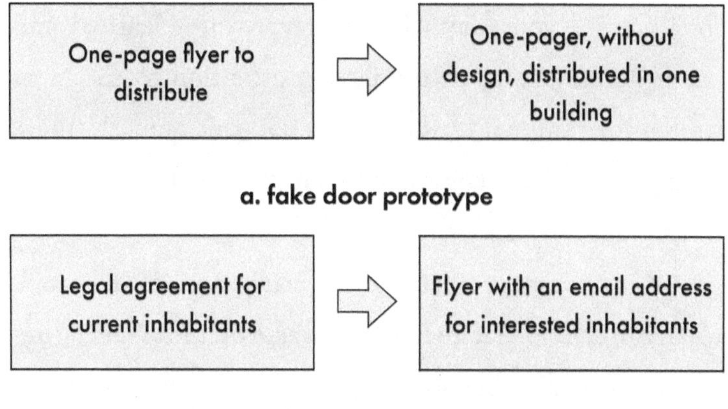

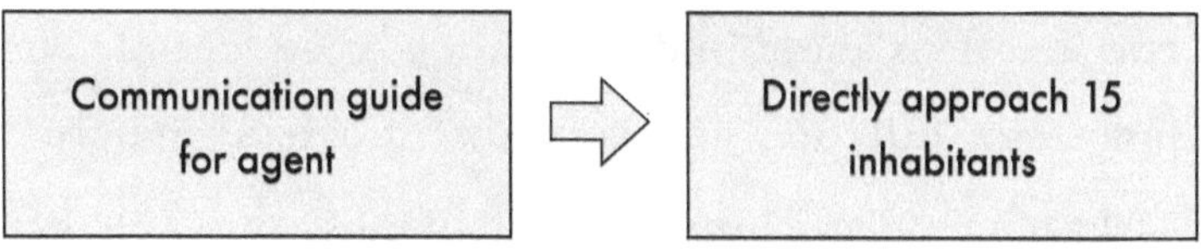

Fig. 21: Strategies to reduce the vertical slice by building prototypes first.

Keep Learning, and Keep Delivering

In this chapter, we discussed how to set a goal, build a map, and follow the process so that you can get started slicing projects on your own. From here, you need to refine and iterate. Refine your plan for the next iteration by updating your map with whatever you've learned, and then iterate again, always paying attention to the most unfamiliar, mission-critical steps. Do this enough times, and you will have completed your project step by step— or, should I say, slice by slice.

But remember: just like the navigators of old, don't plan in detail too far ahead. It's a waste of time. Navigating is an unpredictable journey, no matter what industry you're in. To account for that unpredictability, plan one or two iterations ahead in detail, have a broad idea of your long-term direction and continual progress, and trust that each week will bring you important feedback so that you can continue to adjust course as necessary.

More than anything, trust yourself. You're the captain now, and you know everything you need to know to set sail. Will you make mistakes along the way? Almost certainly. The good news? You'll catch them early. When that happens, trust the process, take what you've learned, and keep moving forward. After all, there's no greater teacher than your own experience.

> **Your Slicing Cheat Sheet**
>
> Ready to apply the approaches in this chapter? Go to https://slicingwork.com/cheat-sheet to download a one-pager that offers a quick overview of these processes.

Conclusion

Congratulations on completing this book!

By seeing how different teams address their projects, you've trained your brain to apply the principles of slicing to different working environments—and to become more adaptable. More importantly, you've learned to focus on what matters when unpredictability occurs.

Long plans don't matter. Results do. Now that you understand this, you and your teams will be better equipped to keep your eyes on the prize and remain disciplined as you work through each project.

And make no mistake, slicing work *is* about discipline.

Often, people think concepts like slicing—which promote agility or adaptive ways of working—allow you to be highly undisciplined. In my experience as both an entrepreneur and a consultant, I've found the opposite is true. There is nothing more undisciplined than facing unpredictability with a traditional, detailed-oriented project management plan and watching it fall apart.

Slicing is not an excuse to abandon structure. Instead, slicing creates a different structure, one that enables us to be resilient *and* disciplined when facing unpredictability.

Now that you've reached the end of the book, you've also learned to focus on delivering results and learning from them. You understand how this way of working affects your team members' sense of ownership and your organization's ability to learn, improve, track progress, ensure quality, and prioritize the highest-value components of a project. Finally, you know that you can apply this new skill in any industry and in projects of any size.

It's time to bring all that knowledge to your own work, so here are some farewell tips to take with you.

Make Looking for Unpredictability a Habit

Whenever you set out to begin a new project, ask yourself these questions:

- Is there any unpredictability I can expect?
- If so, where does that unpredictability come from?

If you're unsure where to expect unpredictability, ask some follow-up questions, such as these:

- Does my project involve changing people's behaviors, perceptions, or opinions?
- What is the technologically new thing I am doing? For instance, am I combining two existing things, introducing technology in a new spot, or something else?
- Are there competitors, partners, or other actors who might change in a way that requires my business to adapt?

These questions will help you anticipate unpredictability in your project—just be careful not to circumvent unpredictability by defining your goals too narrowly. Make sure your goals clearly state your intended outcome for a project. For instance:

- Don't say your goal is to build a software tool when your real goal is to use that tool to change internal processes.
- Don't say you are creating a new process handbook when your real goal is to reduce the time your teams spend on wasteful activities.

Once you have clearly defined your goal and are clear on the impact you want to create, you can then begin to apply what you learned in Chapter 8 (e.g., map the outcomes and slices, prioritize the unfamiliar, slice smaller).

Test Your Slices

When practiced correctly, vertical slicing enables you to learn, adapt, and apply your new knowledge quickly so that you can still produce your target result. Just make sure that what you've created is actually a vertical slice.

To check that you've properly sliced your work, ask the following questions with your team:

- What is going to be different for our customers, or outsiders, once we are done?
- How will they know that anything has changed? What will they see or hear? What will be different?

If you and your team can answer these questions, then that piece of work is typically vertical. If you can't answer these questions, then it's likely you haven't sliced your work properly.

When that happens, consider how you can rephrase or reconsider how you're slicing your work. Often, you'll have the right idea, but if that idea isn't well stated, you won't be able to learn from the result.

The Plan Is Never the Point

If the final result of all your hard work is a plan or a concept, then an alarm bell should go off in your head. (It does for me.)

If that happens, that's not slicing. That's just traditional project management.

You can't learn and get valuable feedback on a concept. You *can* learn or get feedback by creating something that can be tried out.

Don't Let Too Much Time Go By

If the thought of delivering a high-quality piece of work in a short amount of time makes you uncomfortable because you're used to having several months or longer just to plan, you're not alone. Often, leaders new to slicing worry that they won't be able to deliver anything in such a short amount of time.

Trust me, you can.

Don't let too much time go by without delivering something and verifying that you're making progress. Challenge yourself and the people you work with to deliver something within one to two weeks—three to four at most. This can be hard at first, but ultimately it's quite rewarding.

For examples of practices to help you deliver quality outcomes more quickly, see Chapter 7.

Ensure Feedback from Day One

Whatever gets feedback gets improved—but the longer you wait to seek critical feedback, the harder it becomes. So to succeed in a slicing-based model, make sure you set up feedback infrastructure.

Again, this idea may sound difficult if you're accustomed to a more traditional approach. You may wonder how you can get meaningful feedback if you haven't yet produced anything worth knowing. But you'll find that getting and receiving feedback frequently is more valuable and less emotional than getting and receiving it only at the end of a project.

To set up feedback infrastructure, let yourself be led by the outcomes you identify for your slices. Once you know what outcome to expect, you know whom to invite to check whether your slices are working as intended.

If giving and receiving honest feedback isn't a common trait in your organization, please see Chapter 5 for ideas on how to set up an environment where feedback is both welcome and expected from the outset.

Own the Result

In traditional organizations, a person's responsibility is very much defined by their role. So when something goes wrong, there is often a lot of finger-pointing. Who hasn't done their job right? Who hasn't performed in their role?

In organizations that practice slicing, you don't dwell too much on these questions when something goes wrong. That's not where your attention goes; it instead goes toward fixing the problem. So make sure to emphasize your team's responsibility for the final result.

Create Allies

You can't create change in your organization alone. Working on slices instead of focusing on roles and project management is a big shift—one that's much, much easier to manage when you are not alone. So your close coworkers and teammates need to want to realize this change too.

To enlist your coworkers and teammates as allies, share. Share the challenges your company has faced with following outdated plans. Share your frustrations with the way things have been. Share your vision, your ideas, and examples from this book—or even share the book itself.

Then, look for those coworkers whose eyes light up. These are the people who will be essential allies down the long road of advocating for and planning your transition to a new way of working.

You Can't Control What Happens, But You Can Control How You React

This final lesson applies not only to any slicing-based project, but also to your own journey learning this new skill.

If the concepts in this book are new to you, don't expect to be an expert right away. Give yourself time to apply what you've learned, and then revisit what you've done an hour, a day, or even a week later.

Be prepared to completely redo everything, if necessary—and trust that doing so won't be a waste of time. Be patient, and be humble. Don't be too hard on yourself if something goes wrong. No one is an expert at anything the first time they try it. Just like any art, it may not take long to learn the basics of slicing, but it can take a lifetime to perfect the practice.

The Future Is Yours

Imagine a world of work where we acknowledge unpredictability, where we expect it to occur, and where we are honest about our not-knowing. Imagine your team members owning more of their results and being genuinely interested in their impact. Imagine when a failure to achieve an outcome is not a tragedy but an opportunity for more clarity on how to change direction.

Imagine the amount of honesty in such a workplace. Imagine how many more people would actually enjoy working there.

This is not a utopia. It is achievable—and slicing work can bring us much closer to this reality. I know because I've experienced it in action.

If you decide to adopt the art of slicing in your own workplace, I would love to help you, to hear how that journey goes for you, or to offer any pointers if I can. If you have questions or observations about anything in this book—or if you just want to reach out and share a big win with me—you can reach me at anton@slicingwork.com.

You can also visit my website, www.slicingwork.com, and sign up to have regular updates on the art of slicing delivered through my newsletter. I will continually update the website with useful tips, additional resources, and answers to common questions.

Thank you for reading. Now, let's work together to bring the art of slicing to the world.

Acknowledgments

I extend my heartfelt gratitude to those who, knowingly or unknowingly, played a role in the creation of this book:

My profound thanks to Ken Schwaber, Jeff Sutherland, and the Scrum pioneers for establishing and popularizing a framework that laid the foundation for this book through its community and examples.

Special acknowledgment to Jeff McKenna, Henrik Kniberg, Olaf Lewitz, and others at Scrum Alliance® for inspiring my storytelling skills in complex contexts through their exemplary narratives and metaphors.

I am deeply grateful to Steve Blank, Eric Ries, Ash Maurya, Alexander Osterwalder, and colleagues in the Lean Startup movement for fueling my own journey in creating lean organizations—and applying these concepts to new areas outside of business creation.

To David Link, my friend and cofounder, I owe immense gratitude for your inspiration and support during the early phases of my leadership journey.

Special mention to Richard Lawrence from Humanizing Work for his "Work Guide on Splitting User Stories," a perspective I've embraced and extended beyond product development.

My colleagues and friends, Dr. Timon Fiddike and Olaf Lewitz, deserve heartfelt thanks for significantly influencing my thinking and helping me refine my methodologies.

To all my training participants and others who have enriched my narratives and sharpened my insights through their experiences, I am immensely thankful.

My family, for providing the resources, unwavering support, and belief in my pursuits that have been my foundation.

Special thanks to Dr. Timon Fiddike, Gabriel Schüßler, Olaf Lewitz, and Sebastian Kamilli for their invaluable feedback and thorough review of my manuscript.

And to everyone else who has contributed to this journey, your impact, though not named here, is deeply valued.

About the Author

Anton Skornyakov was trained as a mathematician and physicist before pivoting his career to entrepreneurship and business coaching. A Certified Scrum Trainer® for the Scrum Alliance®, he is passionate about improving organizational collaboration and leveraging Agile principles in the public and nonprofit sectors.

This passion led to his current role as cofounder and managing director of Agile.Coach GmbH & Co. KG, where he has coached nearly a hundred organizations and thousands of people in the art of slicing work. This book represents the sum total of all those stories, lessons, and principles.

Anton lives in Berlin, Germany, with his two children.